Politics Goes to the Movies
Hollywood, Europe, and Beyond

Robert P. Kolker

LONDON AND NEW YORK

First published 2018
by Routledge
2 Park Square, Milton Park, Abingdon, Oxon OX14 4RN

and by Routledge
711 Third Avenue, New York, NY 10017

Routledge is an imprint of the Taylor & Francis Group, an informa business

© 2018 Robert P. Kolker

The right of Robert Kolker to be identified as author of this work has been asserted by him in accordance with sections 77 and 78 of the Copyright, Designs and Patents Act 1988.

All rights reserved. No part of this book may be reprinted or reproduced or utilised in any form or by any electronic, mechanical, or other means, now known or hereafter invented, including photocopying and recording, or in any information storage or retrieval system, without permission in writing from the publishers.

Trademark notice: Product or corporate names may be trademarks or registered trademarks, and are used only for identification and explanation without intent to infringe.

British Library Cataloguing-in-Publication Data
A catalogue record for this book is available from the British Library

Library of Congress Cataloging-in-Publication Data
A catalog record for this book has been requested

ISBN: 978-0-415-78761-1 (hbk)
ISBN: 978-0-415-78762-8 (pbk)
ISBN: 978-1-315-22582-1 (ebk)

Typeset in Sabon
by Swales & Willis Ltd, Exeter, Devon, UK

Contents

List of figures	vii
Introduction	1
1 Populism, race, and *The Birth of a Nation* (1915)	9
2 Revolution!: *Battleship Potemkin* (1925)	24
3 Leni Riefenstahl and "Fascinating Fascism": *Triumph of the Will* (1935)	38
4 American democracy and Frank Capra: *Mr. Smith Goes to Washington* (1939)	48
5 Revolution in the 1960s: *The Battle of Algiers* (1966)	59
6 Revolutionary cinema in Latin America: *Lucía* (1968)	70
7 Politics and the apocalypse: *Weekend* (1967)	81
8 Reflections on Fascism: *The Conformist* (1970)	93
9 The Cold War, part one: science fiction and *Invasion of the Body Snatchers* (1956)	102

10 The Cold War, part two: *Point of Order* (1964) and *Dr. Strangelove or: How I Learned to Stop Worrying and Love the Bomb* (1964)   111

11 Hollywood and the blacklist: *Salt of the Earth* (1954)   120

12 Paranoia and political assassination: *JFK* (1991)   130

13 Contemporary American politics: documentaries   139

14 Contemporary American politics: new channels   149

Bibliography   159
Index   163

Figures

1.1	The first campaign film: William McKinley takes a walk with an aide in front of his house in this brief film from 1896	10
1.2	The speculator in wheat is buried in his own product in D. W. Griffith's *Corner in Wheat*	12
1.3	Meanwhile, the farmer quietly goes about his business of sowing seed	12
1.4	A quiet moment of contemplation before the Civil War rages (*The Birth of a Nation*)	15
1.5	The Civil War, as recreated by D. W. Griffith	15
1.6	Griffith's view of the Reconstruction legislature	16
1.7	The ride of the Klan	17
1.8	Revolt of the slaves in Nate Parker's 2016 *The Birth of a Nation*	22
2.1	*Battleship Potemkin*: the shattering of the plate	30
2.2	"Suddenly"	32
2.3	Soldiers shoot down the woman and her wounded child	33
2.4	The woman and the baby carriage	34
2.5	The woman shot in the eye	34
3.1	The intensity of dedication: the drummer boy in *Triumph of the Will*	42
3.2	March through the stadium (*Triumph of the Will*)	44
4.1	Reverence at the Lincoln Memorial in *Mr. Smith Goes to Washington*	52
4.2	Boss Taylor (Edward Arnold) threatens Jeff Smith	53

4.3	A moment of doubt: Jeff (Jimmy Stewart) and Saunders (Jean Arthur) in the shadows of the Lincoln Memorial	54
4.4	At his wit's end during his filibuster, Jeff tosses the telegrams demanding he give up. Senator Paine (just glimpsed in the left background) will soon break down and admit his complicity	55
5.1	Life on the streets in the neorealist film *Bicycle Thieves*	62
5.2	Ali le Pointe (Brahim Hadjadj) and his group of Resistance fighters hide behind a wall that is about to be blown up by the French military	63
5.3	The people of Algiers emerge *en masse* to reclaim their country	67
6.1	The three Lucías: cradled in Fernandina's hands after stabbing Rafael at the end of the 1895 episode (Raquel Revuelta)	75
6.2	Distraught after the loss of Aldo at the end of the 1932 episode (Eslinda Núñez)	77
6.3	Struggling for her rights at the end of the contemporary episode (Adela Legrá)	79
7.1	*Weekend*: the traffic jam	87
7.2	Automobile apocalypse	88
7.3	End of cinema: serving up a meal of some tourist and Corinne's husband	91
8.1	*The Conformist*: Marcello Clerici (Jean-Louis Trintignant) gives the fascist salute while recounting Plato's myth of the cave in the shadows of his professor's room	96
8.2	"Slaughter and melancholy": Clerici visits his father, a fascist now confined in an asylum	99
8.3	Clerici looks back at his own false memories at the end of *The Conformist*	100
9.1	Robby the Robot in *Forbidden Planet*	106
9.2	Miles Bennell (Kevin McCarthy) discovers the simulacrum of his friend in *Invasion of the Body Snatchers*	107
9.3	Miles reacts to the discovery that his girlfriend Becky (Dana Wynter) has become a pod person	108

10.1	"At long last . . . have you left no sense of decency?": Joseph McCarthy, Roy Cohn, and Joseph Welsh in *Point of Order*	113
10.2	The face of nuclear madness: General Ripper (Sterling Hayden) explains his concern over his precious bodily fluids in *Dr. Strangelove or: How I Learned to Stop Worrying and Love the Bomb*	115
10.3	Peter Sellers as Group Capt. Lionel Mandrake, trying to reason with Ripper	116
10.4	Peter Sellers as President Merkin Muffley, talking to the Russian Premier	117
10.5	Fascism is reborn in the War Room: Peter Sellers as Dr. Strangelove	118
11.1	Solidarity: after fighting off the police, the women resume their demonstration for equality in *Salt of the Earth*	127
11.2	"We want the formula!": the jailed women demand food for Esperanza's baby	128
12.1	"We're through the looking glass . . .": Jim Garrison (Kevin Costner), the light shining on his glasses as if to echo his comment, talks to his assistants in *JFK*	135
12.2	An image of the possibly faked *Life* cover picture of Lee Harvey Oswald	135
13.1	Guerilla filmmaking: Michael Moore attempts to waylay a Congressman to see if he would sign up his own son to fight in Iraq (*Fahrenheit 9/11*)	141
13.2	Robert McNamara talks to President Lyndon Johnson in this clip from Errol Morris's *Fog of War*	142
13.3	"If it doesn't fit, you must acquit": at his trial, O. J. Simpson shows off the ill-fitting gloves found at the murder scene (*O. J.: Made in America*)	147
14.1	Selina Meyer (Julia Louis-Dreyfus) and her "body man," Gary (Tony Hale), in *Veep*	150
14.2	Francis Underwood (Kevin Spacey) addresses us during his inauguration	152
14.3	Morgan Freeman makes a guest appearance with the Secretary of State (Téa Leoni) on *Madam Secretary*	154

14.4 John McCain (Ed Harris) introduces his running mate, Sarah Palin (Julianne Moore), in *Game Change*   155

14.5 Lyndon Johnson (Bryan Cranston) confers with Martin Luther King (Anthony Mackie) in *All The Way*   156

Introduction

Politics and ideology

"Politics" embraces a variety of meanings, feelings, actions, and even states of mind. Politics are personal and global, from as direct as a candidate wanting your vote, to a dangerous international crisis, to your own personal life and its relationships. Politics can be a way of looking at the world: conservative or liberal; reactionary or progressive. Politics can speak to optimism or pessimism, can be a source of anger or hope. Politics can be ignored: "I'm not political," some people may say. Politics can identify the views and aspirations of a minority group: "identity politics." Politics can be controlling, even if ignored. Like it or not, wherever we are, we live our lives under a political system that determines everything from the taxes we pay to the medical treatment we receive. These systems protect us by providing rules, regulations, and safeguards, or oppress us by making rules and regulations that restrict our activities and potential. Politics guide the decisions we make; they make up a belief structure as well as an external structure of rules and regulations.

Politics can be personal, not only in the sense of whether we adopt liberal or conservative ideas, but in how those ideas, consciously or not, guide our actions and relationships. "Consciously or not" is the key phrase. We act politically whenever there are issues involving power and the recognition of others. We have heard a lot about "political correctness." The term was initiated in the 1960s as a kind of joke. People on the left asked one another if they were "politically correct" in their beliefs and actions. The term then morphed to mean, broadly, thinking and speaking kindly about other people, particularly minorities. It was then coopted by the right and is now used negatively. To be against "political correctness" means talking tough, even brutally, without regard to people's or a nation's feelings and beliefs.

To be "politically correct" is to be a liberal wimp. Political correctness has become political mockery.

Ideology

Politics is, as you see, a complex business. Almost anything that has to do with the way we interact with other people, in the public or private sphere, can have a political aspect. Voicing an opinion; taking a side; the attitudes we may have toward race and gender, toward immigrants—all of this is political. But because we still tend to think of politics in the large, general sense of elections and elected officials, we need to dig a bit deeper, because there is something that drives the political and forms our beliefs. Driving the larger or more intimate notions of politics, on the macro or micro level, is the concept of ideology. Ideology is a contested, indeed a loaded, term. In popular usage it refers to something "they" have and we don't: "we" are free of ideology, because ideology is something foreign and dangerous. Communism or Fascism are ideologies. Liberal democracy, which embraces the basic concepts of individual liberty and the freedom to rise economically despite class or race, is rarely considered an ideology, perhaps because it is the reigning ideology of many Western countries. But in fact, ideology, the ways in which we see the world, understand, and act in it, the ways in which we consent to the requirements of society and our peers, the opinions we hold, all constitute ideology. When we assent to the ideas and desires of a social group or a national imperative; whether we salute the flag or believe that we should go to college in order to get a good job; if we believe we should vote for a President or a particular party and make a choice about who or what party to vote for; whether we obey the law (or not), we are enmeshed in ideology. Ideology is constituted and in turn constitutes the way we see and agree to the ideas we hold about our world. The Marxist philosopher Louis Althusser wrote:

> It is indeed a peculiarity of ideology that it imposes (without appearing to do so, since these are "obviousnesses") obviousnesses as obviousnesses, which we *cannot fail to recognize* and before which we have the inevitable and natural reaction of crying out (aloud or in the "still, small voice of conscience"): "That's obvious! That's right! That's true."

Ideology, Althusser points out, is a cultural and political "hailing" device. It "hails" us into its obviousness. It assures us that what we think is true and appropriate. It allows us—perhaps drives us—to belong.[1]

But it is not exact to refer to ideology as an "it," as if "it" were something out there, removed from ourselves and our culture. Ideology is the collective and individual sense of the rightness of actions and beliefs, whatever we or our culture takes for granted, takes as true, including truth itself, including our belief systems or our personal sense of ethics and morality. Politics are a major constituent of ideology, ideology in action, the power of ideology that we embrace or reject. Politics is power. If a political candidate, like Bernie Sanders in the 2016 U.S. presidential race, called for "revolution," he was proposing an extraordinary change in the ideology that would drive progressive politics to a radical modification of capitalism (part of liberal democracy, the reigning ideology of the U.S.). On the opposite side, Donald Trump wanted to "make America great again," the supposition being that the country has lost its way, become less than great. An ideology of resentment, fear, and anger drives a politics of strong authority that will somehow move the country and its culture backwards to an imagined better time. The Brexit vote in the U.K. likewise expressed an ideology of nationalistic self-protection that was driven by a politics of bitter division and false promises that offered a purer (and ultimately poorer), more homogenous country, free of foreign influences.

The critic Terry Eagleton suggests that a definition of ideology would embrace "any kind of intersection between belief systems and political power."[2] What we believe, individually or as a group, and how that belief is put into action by ourselves or others constitutes ideology. I would modify this and reverse the terms, suggesting that political power exists at the intersection of ideology and action, both of which include overlapping belief systems. When we select a candidate to receive our vote or react positively or negatively to a racial group or gender identity that is different from our own, we are following the propulsion of ideology and politics. We believe and act or we believe and simply agree or disagree. Assent or disagreement is a passive form of political action; passivity is ideology at rest, not absent. To be political is to be alive within the envelope of ideology. We can delegate political action to others or we can take action based on our ideological beliefs. No matter the variable, actions will be taken and power will be exercised or taken away.

To make matters more interesting, we can think about the differences between political ideology and ideology-driven politics. Political ideology might be described as party affiliation: Republican or Democrat, Conservative or Labor, Right or Left. Ideology-driven politics are more encompassing: Communism, Socialism, Liberal Democracy, Democratic Socialism, Fascism, White Supremacist. These are life-driving beliefs that go beyond who you might vote for and determine the way you view the world and interact with people. This is all to say that politics and ideology are complex, interlocking, shifting forces in our lives and, as we will soon see, in our movies.

Ideology, politics, and culture

Culture encompasses the entirety of who we are, how we act, and what we like as individuals within society. Culture is not uniform. There are many subcultures—just think of the range of musical tastes, tastes in movies, and even more profoundly, gender preferences, and racial or ethnic identity. Each subculture has its own community, its own relationship with the dominant culture, and its particular relationship to the dominant ideology. Ideology, politics, and culture are not interchangeable, but they are deeply embedded one in the other. Any given subculture may practice a variety of politics, though some are more prominent than others. Listeners to country music may tend toward conservative politics. Listeners to National Public Radio are perhaps more liberal than others. But stereotyping, like I have just done in those two sentences, is a kind of politics of simplified classification, driven by a self-assured ideology that pushes me into "obvious" conclusions.

The discussions that take place in this book embrace the triad of ideology, culture, and politics. I will discriminate between them, though sometimes they tend to merge with blurred boundaries. What we believe, how we act on what we believe, what we like, who we like, how the art that we like affects us, how the art that we like or dislike addresses the world around us—all are part of the investigation of movies and politics.

Politics and the movies

We tend to make a sharp distinction between what we consider to be "entertainment" and what we consider to be serious pursuits, like politics (despite the fact that electoral politics are often something like farce). Can the latest superhero movie or romantic comedy have political import; can they be part of our ideological makeup? Doesn't the very notion of "entertainment" promise an escape from daily concerns, global terrors, personal anxieties—even if we watch a zombie movie or a film about terrorism? Perhaps there is something like a sliding scale from films totally divorced from any political or ideological mark to films that specifically address political issues: *Pulp Fiction*

Introduction 5

(Quentin Tarantino, 1994), for example, on one side; *Bridge of Spies* (Steven Spielberg, 2015) on the other. Tarantino's film is a mashup of gangster and buddy films, a comedy with bloodshed, a non-linear narrative of the various adventures of odd, foulmouthed troublemakers. Spielberg's film is a solid, well-made Cold War thriller, a retro look at the early 1960s and the tensions that existed between the U.S. and the Eastern European bloc. The two films could not be more different, but each has political implications.

The politics of Spielberg's films are right on the surface. It tells a story about the CIA working to free Francis Gary Powers, the U2 spy pilot shot down over Russia in 1960, which became a major event in U.S. and U.S.S.R. relations. The film's star, Tom Hanks, playing an unwilling recruit to arrange the transfer of spies in order to free Powers, creates his usual ingratiating performance. The film, while visually dark and foreboding, doesn't leave us in doubt about the outcome or, especially, the anti-Communist perspective (or ideology) that drives it. *Bridge of Spies* confirms the Cold War with all its attendant anxieties; it is a history lesson and perhaps a caution about the existing threats that continue to exist in a troubled world. The film is expressly *about* politics and *is* political in its insistence that the Cold War was worth fighting. We will be looking at films from the Cold War later on.

Pulp Fiction is many things: an homage to Martin Scorsese's early film, *Mean Streets* (1973), and Stanley Kubrick's *The Killing* (1956), both dealing with petty criminals, and, in Kubrick's case, experimenting with a complex non-linear timeline. *Pulp Fiction* attempts to be playful and bloody at the same time; it is nonchalant, profane, and serious only in its attempt to mix up its narrative so that events overlap and occur out of sequence. How then is it political? For one thing, it "hails" the viewer into its jokey, casually violent demeanor, appealing to a particular mindset, even a particular age group to which it introduced its non-traditional subject matter and storytelling. In alluding to a number of genres and films, it depends on an audience schooled in popular culture and ready to take part in the film's lack of serious intent as it rummages around various genres. *Pulp Fiction* also plays on the surfaces of race and gender, positing a friendship between a white man, Vincent (John Travolta), and the African-American Jules (Samuel L. Jackson). It makes homophobic jokes which are difficult to parse as serious or ironic. All in all, despite its innate contradictions, the film became a cultural phenomenon, extremely popular particularly with a cross-section of young adult filmgoers.

There is something more to the political aspect of *Pulp Fiction*. Tarantino's experimentation with form, his use of a non-linear narrative, while not wildly innovative, indicates an important aspect of our study: the politics, even the ideology, of form. Film has power over us. If a typical film works the way in which it was intended, it "hails" us into its story and we may forget our surroundings, our particular concerns. We can become lost in it, allowing it to take over our consciousness. In a sense, we give ourselves up to the movie. If, at the same time, the movie speaks to us about commonplaces like the redemption of an errant man, the value of family above everything, the inevitability of marriage; if it tells us that rich people aren't really happy and that we should follow our dreams, then we are caught in the web of the dominant ideology—bland "obviousnesses" that attempt to be universally applicable. If a film speaks to us about corrupt corporations or politicians, it may be, superficially, moving against the dominant ideology, though still "hailing" us into our commonplace complaints that corporations are corrupt and so are some politicians. Even dystopic films about a bad future or alternative universe can lull us into quiet acceptance. *The Hunger Games* (Francis Lawrence, 2013, 2014, 2015) made a star of Jennifer Lawrence but did not foment anyone outside the film to revolution.

We call conventional filmmaking the Classical Hollywood Style. This includes seamless editing so that the fragments that are filmed in discrete scenes, usually out of narrative order, are put together to create the illusion of a continuous story; "realistic" characters, who are created to have a past and future as well as a present; music that generates emotions; and a careful closure in which all loose narrative ends are put together. In short, an invisible style that does not intrude and that radiates commonplaces. When the style is disrupted, as it is to some extent in *Pulp Fiction*, we are pulled out of the trance, we become conscious of the formal elements of the film, the politics of viewership; the power of the film over us has shifted.

In the course of this book, we will look at a variety of films that play with narrative form, that disrupt the viewing experience, and that speak to politics both directly and indirectly from a variety of perspectives and nationalities. We will look at films that come from the right and the left, that are revolutionary, apocalyptic, or that celebrate the status quo. While we concentrate on the overtly or covertly political, it remains important to understand that all films are political, all speak to power subtly or directly, or have power over us; that they are not innocent. Neither are we. But the aim here is not to ruin entertainment. The films addressed in this book are enormously entertaining, though some in ways you might not be used to. All of them have something to say about our political beliefs, some speak to ideologies foreign or repugnant to ours, and some emerge from different cultures with different experiences of politics and the ideologies that drive them. Come to them with an open mind and your assumptions about what movies can do will be changed.

The choice of films

I have made a wide-ranging and somewhat personal choice of films that, with some exceptions (*The Birth of a Nation, Triumph of the Will*), I both admire and enjoy. These films cover a wide spectrum of film history and nationalities—American, European, and Latin American—and an array of political/ideological positions, from Fascism to democracy to Communism. Films that address the politics of race and gender are also included. Not all nationalities and not every moment or decade in film history is covered, but rather those that seem to provide a solid base for analysis and for further exploration. Also, all of these films are made with a pressure to expose, reveal, even change the political status quo. Some are merely didactic: they want to teach us something about politics. Others are propagandistic. Some burn with a passion for political change.

I have broken the discussion into units, most of them focusing on one film, though in some instances, where there are important interconnections, I have included other films to round out the analysis. In the last chapters of the book, I discuss television films and series. There is little doubt that some of the most interesting political films are now made for cable or streaming on TV or other devices. This should be cause for neither concern nor praise, but rather an understanding that the locus of important filmmaking is in the process of shifting screens. While we speak of films that ask us to take an active interpretive role, we remain in many ways at the mercy of the movie production system, which has undergone many changes over the years. Films, even political films that may attack the sources of money, cost a lot of money to make, and money is now made back on films and programs made for home consumption. There is certainly a lot of convenience built into this and also a strong necessity. *O. J.: Made in America* (Ezra Edelman, 2016), arguably the most trenchant film ever made concerning race, is six and a half hours long. It would not be possible to present this in a movie theater. Broken into episodes, television broadcast becomes its best medium for exhibition. And, at the moment, television—network, cable, streaming—is the best medium for experimentation. Theatrical films have become a bit sclerotic, unwilling to experiment with form or content. The intimate space of the personal screen appears to be the most conducive to thoughtful works about politics.

Whatever the venue, films that address politics and films that are made politically challenge us to combine entertainment with a wider view of the world and its machinations, its ideologies—the visual representation of the ways our lives are lived, constructed—and, perhaps, to fight back against oppression.

Notes

1 Louis Althusser, "Ideology and Ideological State Apparatuses," *Lenin and Philosophy*, trans. Ben Brewster (New York and London: Monthly Review Press, 1971), 172, 173.
2 Terry Eagleton, *Ideology* (London and New York: Verso, 1991), 6.

1 Populism, race, and *The Birth of a Nation* (1915)

We start with a film that encapsulates many of the issues discussed in the Introduction, but with an added burden: it is a silent film made in 1915, and it is racist to its very core. To understand the film, we need to put it in the context of when it was made, who made it, how it was received, and what we can do with it now. We need also to consider if we can solve a fundamental, indeed universal problem of what to do with a work of art whose politics are abhorrent.

Movies began as a novelty, one of the many technological inventions of the 19th century, though, at the time, not seen as important as the railroad, the telegraph, photography, or the electric light bulb. These inventions were all about time and space. The railroads allowed people to move relatively quickly across wide areas. Telephony, which included long-distance communication by Morse code and then voice, collapsed space; it also led to radio, which by the early 20th century brought news, entertainment, and music into the home. Electricity, which made radio and telephony possible, not only linked small and large areas, but the light bulb extended time itself. Photography froze time in visual space. Night was no longer the time of withdrawal and sleep, but of continued activity. Movies combined these phenomena of modernity, creating in effect a time and space machine where viewers— first in storefront peepshows and later in ornate picture palaces—could see versions of their worlds, see *more* of their worlds, become absorbed in the fictions of assent.

Early movies were very short, a few minutes of action: a strongman flexing his muscles, a woman dancing, workers leaving a factory, a train arriving at a station. These were transnational movies, some made in the U.S. by Thomas Edison, whose workshop, headed by W. K. L. Dickson, developed the process of putting a succession of images on a strip of film and running them through an illuminated viewer, creating the illusion of motion. Others came from France,

10 *Populism, race, and* The Birth of a Nation

where the Lumière Brothers photographed everyday events, making them unusual by the very act of isolating and privileging them on film. And this was the key to the immediate popularity of the movies: creating or recording events, isolating them from the immediate rush of everyday life, and then presenting them to viewers as concentrated, provoking, moving experiences.

Electoral politics entered almost immediately into the catalogue of early films. In 1896, William McKinley, soon to become the 25th President of the United States, was filmed in a very short (just over a minute) movie, walking with an aide across the lawn of his house to receive a piece of paper from another man (Figure 1.1). McKinley was also captured on film during his inauguration and posthumously during the funeral procession following his assassination. But there was more at stake than elections and mourning. Here was the first President to make use of mass media and thus marked movies, from their birth to their maturity and in their current decline, as a voice of politics, ideologies, and the cultures of both the filmmakers and viewers. Politics came to the screen.[1] The McKinley footage presaged newsreels of current events, but it was fiction films that made a lasting mark. One early film stands out as the most potent, politically charged film of the silent period: D. W. Griffith's 1915 epic, *The Birth of a Nation*.

Figure 1.1 The first campaign film: William McKinley takes a walk with an aide in front of his house in this brief film from 1896.

The McKinley film was made by W. K. L. Dickson, the former Edison employee, and shot by cameraman Billy Bitzer. The production company was the American Mutoscope and Biograph Company, a rival to Edison and the beginning of what would become a large number of production and distribution companies competing with each other before the formation of the major studios early in the 20th century. The significance of Biograph (as it was popularly called) was that it became home to one of the most important directors of the silent period, D. W. Griffith. A would-be actor and playwright, Griffith, a son of the South, born in Kentucky to a father who was a Confederate soldier, joined Biograph in 1908. Instead of acting, Griffith became a director. Between 1908 and 1913, when he left to form his own company, he made, with the assistance of cameraman Billy Bitzer and a stock company of actors, some 450 short films.

In the course of this astonishing output, Griffith refined many filmic techniques and became especially adept at two stylistic practices: careful compositions that rendered a striking and eloquent image, and editing together sequences that were each happening at the same time but in different spaces. Griffith used this technique of parallel editing as a means of narrative contrast and tension. Scenes of someone, usually a woman, in a situation of distress or capture are intercut with scenes of a man rushing to her rescue. At the end of this alternation, the rescuer arrives at the person in distress and saves her.

In 1909, Griffith made a fourteen-minute film called *Corner in Wheat*. The story is simple: a capitalist wants to own all the grain produced by farmers. The film—as with all good films—is more interesting than its plot. There are lyrical shots of a farmer sowing his field along with a bakery where the price of bread keeps going up intercut with the capitalist, who schemes to buy up the wheat and the stock exchange where investors bid up the prices. At one point, the farmer returns to his family empty-handed—no money for his labors. In another, a mob comes to the bakery to protest the high prices. The capitalist visits his grain storage facility, falls into the pit, and is buried by his grain pouring down—the last we see of him are his fingers wiggling out of the mountain of grain that is suffocating him. The film ends with his body being pulled out and another shot of the poor farmer, sowing his fields (Figures 1.2 and 1.3).

The film represents a strain of populism that runs strongly through American and European politics, and it is worth examining before we get to *The Birth of a Nation*. Populism is a slippery term. At its base, it is an "us against them" ideology. The poor and the struggling pitted against the wealthy elite. This is different from class struggle,

Figure 1.2 The speculator in wheat is buried in his own product in D. W. Griffith's *Corner in Wheat*.

Figure 1.3 Meanwhile, the farmer quietly goes about his business of sowing seed.

a more complex, left-wing ideology that addresses economic, cultural, and social differences and speaks to oppression and the means—often revolutionary—to overcome it. Populism is most often a right-wing ideology of resentment and fear, an ideology of nationalism, and too often of racism, a reaction to a world that seems to be in control of "elites" and spinning out of control from "ordinary people" who cannot control it. Populism is often darkly apocalyptic about the future while casting a foolish eye on an idealized past that never existed.[2]

This is a bit too heavy a burden to place on Griffith's little film. *Corner in Wheat* is populism writ small, a quiet voice contrasting the rural with the urban, the poor with the rich, the humble with the greedy. It would seem to indicate that Griffith's ideology was soundly in tune with the Progressive Era, which sought an ideal world of equality and morality.[3] But there was a competing ideology at work during the early part of the 20th century. Racism was raging; segregation and violence against African Americans was strong. And Griffith could not resist it. In his signature work, the "other," the African American, became the target of a racist onslaught. In terms of a career move, *The Birth of a Nation* is innocent and compelling enough, the result of Griffith's desire to break free of the length restraints imposed on him by the Biograph company and make longer films. As a result, he made, in *The Birth of a Nation*, the first long-form film in U.S. film history, and he uses its length to cover the period before, during, and after the Civil War. He attempts to contain this historical expanse by focusing on a few families and large battle sequences. The film is notable both for the delicacy with which Griffith portrays the domestic lives of the Southern Cameron family, whose activities provide an anchor for the diverse events of the film, and the large battle panoramas of the Civil War sequences. But the film takes its ugly turn after the war when it attempts to portray Reconstruction, the rebuilding of the South, as a historical disaster, causing the rise of the Ku Klux Klan.

The Birth of a Nation is based on a 1905 novel and play by Thomas Dixon called *The Clansman*. It celebrates the Ku Klux Klan as protectors of white people after the Civil War and the freeing of enslaved people. Dixon's racism was of a piece with, if perhaps a bit more heated than, the reigning ideology of the time, especially in the South. The brief ascendency of African Americans into some political power—they got the vote, they served as state legislators—came to a dismal end when the government withdrew its troops from the Confederate states in 1877. Jim Crow, slavery without actual ownership of people, oppressed African Americans with segregation, humiliation, terrorism, and lynching. The Klan became a potent agent of this terrorism and violence.

Why did Griffith follow suit? It seems that he was little more than an everyday racist of the time, exacerbated by his Southern heritage. Ideologically, this would indicate that he believed in the inferiority of African Americans and was probably sentimental about the "Old South" and its clichés of male honor and female gentility. Understanding this helps us understand why he did *not* make a film that he consciously thought would create the furor and backlash that it did. Yet he took his source material to heart and the racism of his film grows organically, almost *obviously*, from the narrative that Griffith creates. Slavery-Peace-War-Loss-Retribution seems to be the pattern of the film and the ideological narrative of the South itself.

The film begins innocently enough, depicting the friendship of the Camerons in the South and the Stonemans from the North. Ben Cameron, the "Little Colonel" (Henry Walthall), is in love with Elsie Stoneman (Lillian Gish). But the Stonemans are not merely northerners but abolitionists as well—they want the end of slavery. Stoneman himself (played by Ralph Lewis) is modeled after the real-life abolitionist, Thaddeus Stevens, a Republican senator at a time when a faction of Republicans constituted the anti-slavery movement. Griffith's film depicts him as a power-mad dictator. The domestic harmony of the unlikely friendship between the two families and the lovingly portrayed peace of the "Old South" is shattered by the outbreak of the Civil War. The transition is presented in a delicate composition in which "The Little Colonel," having bid goodbye to the Stoneman sons, stands in the right side of the frame, leaning against a pillar, with a long thoughtful look (Figure 1.4). Peace is over.

The transition to depicting the Civil War is done by means of "an historical facsimile" (as the title card reads) of Abraham Lincoln, signing a decree to call up volunteers to defend the North. The film is peppered with these tableaux depicting historical moments involving Lincoln, whom Griffith regards as a somewhat wrong-headed great man. As to the battle, Griffith is quite clever in its representation, alternating large battle tableaux with images of the Stoneman and Cameron brothers, who ultimately die on the battlefield in each other's arms: stirring battle scenes and small, personal episodes alternate in a broad canvas that narrows to ugly bigotry (Figure 1.5).

Up to this point, where the battle sequences all but dwarf everything else, the film's racism is somewhat muted. We see a group of slaves doing a dance during the Stonemans' visit to the Camerons. In Washington, Stoneman's "mulatto" lover goes into spasms of hate when asked to open the door for one of his associates. After the war,

Figure 1.4 A quiet moment of contemplation before the Civil War rages (*The Birth of a Nation*).

Figure 1.5 The Civil War, as recreated by D. W. Griffith.

16 *Populism, race, and* The Birth of a Nation

however, the full canker of racial hatred opens up. There are sequences of the love blooming between the Cameron and Stoneman children, but the moments of cuteness and sentiment are mere diversions from the real focus, which is on Stoneman, who aggregates power by (as the film sees it) turning control over to the freed African Americans, under the leadership of his "mulatto" henchman, the curiously named Silas Lynch (George Siegmann). It is important to note that the leading African-American characters in the film are played by white men in blackface. Racial calumny is mediated in such a way that even its victims are barely allowed to show themselves.

The South Carolina legislature erupts in chaos under African-American rule. The members put their bare feet up on their desks, drink alcohol, and (of course) eat chicken, making a mockery of the legislative process, capped by what Griffith believes is an unspeakable outrage: passing a bill to allow miscegenation (Figure 1.6). But Griffith has even more outrage to come, perhaps the most virulent horror of the racist imagination: rape of a white woman by a black man. Gus, a "renegade" black soldier (a white actor in blackface), stalks the Camerons' daughter, eventually causing her to leap to her death to avoid his clutches. This part of the story is placed in a peaceful pastoral setting, so that the visuals are in contrast to the outrage being portrayed.

Figure 1.6 Griffith's view of the Reconstruction legislature.

Populism, race, and The Birth of a Nation 17

But it is a violent scene nonetheless, and it is meant to exploit the racist fears of its audience.

In the midst of all this, "The Little Colonel" muses over the ruin of the Old South; he sees a group of black children playing. Some of them put a white sheet over themselves and scare away the others. "The inspiration," reads the intertitle, and "The Little Colonel" is inspired to form the Ku Klux Klan. In historical fact, the Klan got started in 1865 by a group of white Confederate soldiers in Tennessee and grew, spreading terror and violence against the African-American citizens of the South.[4] But Griffith's imagination demands a more personal, even sentimental invention of home-grown terrorism. As far as the film is concerned, however, the Klan is born from the family we have been observing—and hopefully identifying with—from the beginning, and its deeds are in the service of rescuing members of both families, Camerons and Stonemans. The ride of the Klan is the climactic moment of white salvation and redemption. They capture, try, and execute the rapist (Figure 1.7).

Things deteriorate from here, and the film suddenly turns into a captivity narrative in which the Cameron family and Stonemans' son are pursued by rampaging African Americans, only to take refuge with Union veterans. A chilling title card reads, "The former enemies

Figure 1.7 The ride of the Klan.

McQueen and Hattie McDaniel, black actresses who early on broke the Hollywood color barrier, though they often had no choice but to take demeaning roles.

Gone with the Wind goes so far as to duplicate a scene from *Birth*. After the war, Scarlett and Mammy take a walk through Reconstruction Atlanta. A pair of well-dressed African Americans walk past, laughing slightly menacingly. Scarlett gives them a quizzical look. Carpetbaggers—whites from the North—make rude remarks about Scarlett. They pass a white man promising, with a cynical tone, "Forty Acres and a Mule." A sign in the background announces the same, which was, in fact, a land offer made by the Federal Government to the freed slaves. The man continues: "Because we're your friends, and you're going to become voters and you're going to vote like your friends do." Gullible black voices call out, "and a mule? . . . Gee!"

The parallel sequence in *The Birth of a Nation* occurs when Stoneman sends his "mulatto" aide, Silas Lynch (leering with lust at Stoneman's daughter), to organize "the power of the negro vote." We see African Americans dancing madly, black Union soldiers marching in the background, and behind them is a sign that reads:

Equality

Equal Rights

Equal Politics

Equal Marriage

Forty Acres and A Mule

For Every Colored Citizen.

The freedmen are given food, and the title card reads, in part: "The charity of a generous North misused to delude the ignorant."

Both films assume the same perverse view of Reconstruction, and the politics of racism are in full view. Somehow, in the view of these films, the freed slaves have been fooled—by their freedom, by the promises of the government, by the corruption of the northerners, by the carpetbaggers, who have come to take advantage of their ignorance, and by the Civil War itself. That "ignorance" is taken for granted and in so doing tries to negate what the Civil War was about and delegitimize the freeing of slaves. The postwar violence depicted in *The Birth of a Nation*, the sentimentality over "the Old South" in *Gone with the Wind*, are acts not only of racism, but of political defiance, *historical* defiance. Part of the definition of politics involves action taken on behalf of a group or society. These films insist that the action of freeing the slaves and helping them achieve equality is actually one that *denies* the rights of white people. The politics and culture of racism and fear, anger and resentment make a potent brew.

The racist ideologies spoken by the two films are in different registers. D. W. Griffith makes full use of the new cinematic stylistics being developed at the time. There are lyrical and sentimental sequences, tableaux of historical moments like the assassination of Lincoln, brilliantly staged battle sequences, and the dynamic action of the ride of the Klan. *Gone with the Wind*, with its many directors and overbearing producer, David O. Selznick, is fully engaged with the Hollywood continuity style. There are no experiments, just a very long seamless narrative of a woman too self-centered to be a part of the brutal history played out but mostly unseen. Only the dramatic crane up over the dead and wounded spread out over the ground in Atlanta offers something indicating cinematic energy. To put it another way, *The Birth of a Nation* blasts its racism loudly through a display of cinematic form that is being created seemingly as we watch. *Gone with the Wind* croons its racism and lulls us into a sentimental torpor that would allow us to forget what it's doing if we don't wake up and pay attention.

There is no question that the racism so blatantly presented in these two films has been somewhat modified, or at least gone underground into the cultural unconscious, coming to the fore when the political atmosphere is open to it. We have, thankfully, become more aware of the history, past and present, of racial attitudes. Laws have been passed, language has shifted, we tend—most of us, at least—not to be vocal about our worst attitudes. Many of us no longer even have those attitudes. The movies have followed suit. As we will see in a later chapter, contemporary film is rarely overtly racist and sometimes *about* race, examining its history and its politics. But it is important to see what film has done in order to appreciate the distance we have come and the distance we have yet to go.

The Birth of a Nation: 2016

It takes a great deal of self-confidence to make a film with the same name as one of the monuments in the history of American cinema. The film should be a powerful response to Griffith's racism and equal or better in its formal invention. Nate Parker's 2016 film is neither.

22 *Populism, race, and* The Birth of a Nation

Figure 1.8 Revolt of the slaves in Nate Parker's 2016 *The Birth of a Nation*.

Rather, it is a competent retelling of the slave rebellion led by Nat Turner in 1831. Parker portrays slavery in all its brutality without dwelling on the violence; his Nat Turner quietly seethes against his owners and his "job" as itinerant slave preacher. The revolt, which takes place near the very end of the film, is doomed from its start, but *necessary*—not only because it is a historical fact, but because the degradation of slavery demanded the representation of courageous individuals standing up against all odds, fighting their owners, and facing a horrible death as a result (Figure 1.8).

The film breaks no new formal ground and, ultimately, has no important relation with its namesake. There were great hopes that it would be an important political and commercial breakthrough for an African-American film made by an African American. It appeared at a point when many were conscious of the lack of such productions. The lack of minority representation in filmmaking had become something of a scandal. The film failed at the box office. Its failure was not due altogether to the film itself. The discovery that its director/star had been charged but acquitted in a rape case some years earlier, and that the victim in the case later committed suicide, soiled the film and influenced its reception.[8]

This raises an important and difficult question, one that parallels the problem of whether a film's politics can be separated from its formal achievement. Can we enjoy D. W. Griffith's *The Birth of a Nation* despite its ugly racism? Can we be aware of formal beauty and blind to repugnant content? I believe we cannot. Abhorrent politics leave a stain on the work that no passage of time can erase. As much as we may admire the energy of Griffith's filmmaking, we keep returning to the poisonous content that energy produces. But can we separate the personal life of the artist from his creation? That question I leave to you.

Notes

1 For an analysis of the McKinley film, see Jonathan Auerbach, "Looking In: McKinley at Home," *Body Shots: Early Cinema's Incarnations* (Berkeley, CA: University of California Press, 2007), 15–41.
2 For definitions of populism, see Noam Gidron and Bart Bonikowski, "Varieties of Populism: Literature Review and Research Agenda," *Working Paper Series, Weatherhead Center for International Affairs* (New Haven, CT: Harvard University, No 12–0004), http://scholar.harvard.edu/files/gidron_bonikowski_populismlitreview_2013.pdf.
3 For the Progressive Period, see Jackson Lears, *Rebirth of a Nation: The Making of Modern America, 1877–1920* (New York: HarperCollins, 2000).
4 For a solid history of the Klan, see www.splcenter.org/sites/default/files/Ku-Klux-Klan-A-History-of-Racism.pdf.
5 The quotation from Woodrow Wilson is from his *A History of the American People*, vol. LX (New York: Harper & Brothers, 1918 [originally published 1901]), 60–65.
6 For the history of the film see Melvyn Stokes, *D. W. Griffith's* The Birth of a Nation*: A History of 'The Most Controversial Motion Picture of All Time'* (New York: Oxford University Press, 2007).
7 See www.aaregistry.org/historic_events/view/lincoln-motion-picture-company-first-black-cinema. For Oscar Micheaux see J. Ronald Green, *Straight Lick: The Cinema of Oscar Micheaux* (Bloomington, IN: University of Indiana Press, 2000).
8 See the essay by Roxane Gay in *The New York Times*: www.nytimes.com/2016/08/21/opinion/sunday/nate-parker-and-the-limits-of-empathy.html.

Further reading

Pearl Bowser, Jane Gaines, Charles Musser, eds., *Oscar Micheaux and His Circle: African- American Filmmaking and Race Cinema of the Silent Era* (Bloomington and Indianapolis, IN: Indiana University Press, 2001).

Thomas Cripps, *Slow Fade to Black: The Negro in American Film, 1900–1942* (New York: Oxford University Press, 1977).

Tom Gunning, *D. W. Griffith and the Origins of American Narrative Film: The Early Years at Biograph* (Urbana and Chicago, IL: University of Illinois Press, 1991).

Jackson Lears, *Rebirth of a Nation: The Making of Modern America, 1877–1920* (New York: Harper Collins, 2009).

Melvyn Stokes, *D. W. Griffith's* The Birth of a Nation*: A History of 'The Most Controversial Motion Picture of All Time'* (New York: Oxford University Press, 2007).

2 Revolution!
Battleship Potemkin (1925)

Political ideology—the lens through which we attempt to clarify and address our world and how it should be governed—encompasses a broad spectrum. On the right, there is an arc from moderate conservative to reactionary and past that into Fascism. On the left, there is an arc from liberal to socialist to Communist. The extreme right and left, totalitarian Fascism and Stalinist Communism, brush against each other. The right spectrum trends from populism to individualism, speaks about less government, unrestricted, unregulated corporate activity, and the preservation of "traditional values." As it approaches Fascism, rather than less government there is a linking of the government and corporate spheres along with a powerful and violent dose of racism and terror, especially against minority groups. The left emphasizes strong government, especially as it provides a safety net for its citizens (in the form of universal medical care, for example). As it moves further along the spectrum, embracing Marxist ideals of "the dictatorship of the proletariat," it becomes less idealist and more authoritarian; rather than the corporation, it holds the state as the most powerful and all-encompassing entity. Hitler was the brutal end of the totalitarian right; Stalin of the totalitarian left.

We will examine Fascism and the way it was represented in film in the next chapter; here we will speak about the Russian Revolution of 1917, and, in particular, how film, which Vladimir Lenin, who moved the Revolution to its success, called its most important art. The philosophical and ideological force behind the Russian Revolution was the works of Karl Marx, who wrote at length about capitalism and its inevitable collapse not only under its own weight, but because of the pressure brought on it by an oppressed working class. Marx drew upon the German philosopher Hegel and the concept of dialectics: a set of opposing ideas, capital and labor, in Marx's view, that would clash and create a third thing, a dominant proletariat. Russia was not a capitalist country, but rather a Tsarist monarchy ruling a huge, largely rural population. Still, the unpopularity of the Tsar and his oppression of his people, the deprivations caused by WWI, an uprising of the military, and an ideologically driven band of revolutionaries led to the overthrow and murder of the Tsar and the establishment of a new society, the USSR, the Union of Soviet Socialist Republics.

The Revolution was much more complex than can be summarized in a single sentence. What is important for us is how the movies played a role in post-revolutionary Russia. And not solely the movies. The energy of the Revolution spilled over and into all the arts. From painting and music to architecture and poetry, experimentation was rife. A new society needed a new art, and the government wanted to make sure everyone knew this. It sent "agitprop" trains across the country to introduce the Revolution in the arts to the populace. For a brief time, the avant-garde flourished.

There were a number of developments in filmmaking that met the challenges of the new society. Dziga Vertov (his real name was Denis Kaufman; his pseudonym means "spinning top") made visual newspapers called *Kino Pravda* that imaginatively addressed the day-to-day lives of the people. His major work, *The Man with the Movie Camera* (1929), is a celebration of the cinema eye and its ability to pierce reality's veil to see the startling workings of reality in the daily world. Dziga Vertov was a fanciful documentarist, exploring the limits of his discipline to activate new perceptions of the new order. Fiction filmmakers, the best known being Lev Kuleshov, Vsevolod Pudovkin, and Sergei Eisenstein, searched for new techniques of telling stories of the Revolution in cinematic form. For all three, the key new techniques lay in editing, and a specific form of editing at that, called montage.

In the preceding chapter, we took note of D. W. Griffith's editing style—parallel editing—in which scenes of someone, usually a woman, in danger is intercut with her male rescuer, or in the case of *The Birth of a Nation*, the Ku Klux Klan, coming to save the day. We also noted *Corner in Wheat*, the short film in which Griffith cuts between rich and poor, a stock manipulator and a farmer. Eisenstein, in his 1944 essay "Dickens, Griffith, and the Film Today," saw the ideological basis of the Griffith style. He compares his theory of montage with Griffith's parallel editing that he and his colleagues studied in detail:

> Montage thinking is inseparable from the general content of thinking as a whole. The structure that is reflected in the concept of Griffith montage is the structure of bourgeois [that is, middle-class] society ... [His style] is woven of irreconcilably alternating

layers of "white" and "red"—rich and poor . . . And this society, perceived *only as a contrast between the haves and the have-nots*, is reflected in the consciousness of Griffith no deeper than the image of an intricate race between two parallel lines.[1]

Eisenstein goes on say that Griffith's montage style is mainly one of "tempo," but his central point remains a political and ideological one: the parallel lines of Griffith's editing structure may, on the level of plot, allow the meeting and rescuing of the captive heroine by the powerful hero or (in the case of the Klan) heroes, but it fails to create the dialectical energy of a new social order, to become more than the rescuing hero and rescued woman. *Corner in Wheat* leaves the farmer quietly planting his seed for the next harvest to be stolen by the next capitalist buying up the market.

Fair enough. Griffith was not a revolutionary. He was a populist at best, a reactionary racist at worst. And the ride of the Klan in *The Birth of a Nation* is a powerful ideological statement about white supremacy. Eisenstein and his colleagues were revolutionaries and they did not want their films to be "perceived only as a contrast between the haves and the have-nots." They wanted their films to reflect revolutionary class struggle and, in Eisenstein's case, to represent Marxist dialectical materialism in visual form. To this end, he and his colleagues reinterpreted Griffith's editing style. To understand this more fully, we need to briefly understand the main building blocks of film.

There are two components to film structure: the shot and the edit or cut. The shot contains everything that goes on in front of the camera, as well as elements added later. This has always been the case in Hollywood filmmaking, though today, with the universal use of computer-generated imagery (CGI), many of the elements of the shot are added after the actors have been photographed; indeed, sometimes the actors themselves are computer generated. The shot is any unedited piece of finished film. Editing is what's done to the shot, which can be cut at any point and attached to another shot to build, indeed create, the film's narrative. (Keep in mind that we are here talking about older ways of filmmaking. Today, most film is shot and all film is edited digitally. The "cut" is rarely a physical act.) What D. W. Griffith and many others were doing in the formative years of American cinema was institutionalizing what has become known as the Classical Hollywood Style or the Hollywood continuity style.[2] This includes invisible cutting, unobtrusive shot composition (though Griffith's compositions are often quite eloquent), and narrative content that depends upon melodramatic or comic events, the posing of some kind of danger to the characters, and resolving that danger through heroic acts, the joining together of a couple, or other acts of resolution and redemption—the ride to the rescue.

The result is an ideology of assent. The Classical Hollywood Style requires a kind of buy-in, a willingness, even in a film like *The Birth of a Nation*, to assent to its unquestioning presentation of white righteousness and an African-American threat. That is why the film is so difficult to take if you don't share its racial views and the way a film whose views you *do* share is so easy to take. The Classical Hollywood Style, to go back to our earlier definition of ideology, seems to say, "That's obvious! That's right! That's true!" Virtue will be rewarded. Enemies will be foiled. Lovers will be united. The evil corporation will be exposed. The hero will be redeemed. And all the while you will be taken through a seamless narrative that renders its form invisible.

The revolutionary Russian filmmakers thought differently. They looked at editing as a means of visual, emotional, and political stimulation. They marveled at the potentials it held to affect the viewer and create the kind of response they felt could not be attained by shot composition alone. The legendary example of this is the so-called "Kuleshov effect." The director Lev Kuleshov took a shot of a closeup of an actor with a fairly neutral expression. He cut it into three pieces and inserted into the cuts a shot of children playing, then a shot of a table with food, and then a corpse in a coffin. According to the legend, the viewers of this montage were delighted with the actor's expression—his joy at seeing the children at play, hunger at the sight of food, and sadness at the image of the deceased.

The Kuleshov effect is a clever trick, and it reveals the conventions of trickery that editing creates. When, in any film, we see an actor reacting to something just said or seen, it is quite possible that the reaction shot was not taken at the same time or even the same place as what was seen or heard. Illusion-making occurs in the shot and across the edit from shot to shot. But illusion was not what Sergei Eisenstein was after. He wanted montage to be an emotional and intellectual weapon; he wanted to move the viewer with the power of one shot colliding with another:

> The leap . . . beyond the *limits of the possibilities* of the stage—a leap beyond the *limits of situation*; a leap into the field of montage *image*, montage *understanding*, montage as means before all else of revealing the *ideological conception*.[3]

That conception, as far as Eisenstein was concerned, was to recreate the energy of the Revolution in the viewer of the film, both on a conscious and unconscious level—with a punch. Dziga Vertov, the documentarist, wanted to create the *kino eye*; Eisenstein wanted to create the *kino fist*.[4]

This tough talk belies the fact that the highest form of montage for Eisenstein was *intellectual* montage—the "ideological conception"—moving the viewer from visceral perception up to the level of political thought. Propaganda, perhaps, but going to the root meaning of the word: the propagating of a political idea. And for Eisenstein, montage was at the root of filmmaking. Though he and his cinematographer, Eduard Tisse, made extraordinary images, they were, for Eisenstein, only the bricks to be joined with other images to create a montage structure, or cell. These cells, further edited together, create the whole film, in what Eisenstein called an organic whole.

It is difficult, given the length of time and the enormous difference in political culture since then, to know exactly how Eisenstein's contemporary audience responded to his films. Were they charged with revolutionary fervor? Did the films affirm their commitment to the new Russia? To make things even more complicated, his films—particularly the one we are most concerned with here—were reedited and parts removed according to the often malevolent political winds of the time. Despite this, they were extremely popular in their time.[5] More important now is how we respond. Do such films make us lean toward an understanding of Marxist dialectics and the historical inevitability of revolution? Probably not, but they remain important examples of revolutionary cinema made in something like revolutionary form. Of the four major films that Eisenstein made in the 1920s—*Strike* (1925), *Battleship Potemkin* (1925), *October: Ten Days That Shook the World* (1928), and *Old and New* (1929)—*Battleship Potemkin* is the best remembered and perhaps the best example of Eisensteinian montage. It deserves a close look.

The film is based on a mutiny aboard a Tsarist ship in 1905, as the Revolution was catching fire. Despite the ultimate failure of the revolt (the ship broke down and landed in Romania, where many of the sailors remained until after the Revolution), it managed, before its failure, to catch the attention and participation of the people of Odessa, whose enthusiasm was put down by the Tsar's army.[6] Eisenstein's adaptation of this "true story" is an exercise in the encapsulation of history within cinematic form. The story of the mutiny aboard the ship Potemkin is completely absorbed and refigured within a new entity called *Battleship Potemkin* in which the mutiny is successful. It is absorbed so thoroughly that history drops out and is largely forgotten, while Eisenstein's film has become not only a monument in film history, but a lesson in political form.

The first part of the film is called "Of Men and Maggots," the latter referring to the rancid meat served to the sailors that initiates their revolt. Early on, we see the men sleeping in their hammocks below deck. An ordinary representation of this scene would most likely consist of a shot of the men in their hanging slings at close quarters with, perhaps, some closeups cut in. Eisenstein emphasizes the closeness of the quarters by presenting the sleeping men in a tight shot that allows no space between them. What's more, their hammocks are slung at severe angles to one another, swinging back and forth, creating an almost abstract pattern of diagonals. Eisenstein cuts to create a rhythm of diagonal lines that he calls "a conflict between colliding shots."[7] This conflict of forms is the basis of all Eisensteinian montage, and the hammocks are the most dramatic introduction to what will be a constantly shifting rhythm of shots that will increase in complexity as the film moves on.

One aspect of montage is its ability to manipulate time. Obviously, all movies do this, compressing a long period of time into two hours or less. It is essential that the Classical Hollywood Style create an invisible temporal continuity, to, in effect, make time disappear. It is in the nature of Eisensteinian montage to protract time in ways that break continuity rules. Revolution is, in part, a fracturing of history's time as an old regime and its ideology gives way, often violently, to a new one. Eisenstein figures this in breaking up time within a montage, thereby breaking continuity in service of forcing audience attention. This can be something as subtle as breaking the continuity of an ordinary action: in the sailor's mess, an officer descends the stairs. In the first shot, he descends to the bottom of the steps. In the second shot, taken at a further distance, he descends again. Time is doubled.

A little later in the sequence, a group of sailors are washing dishes. One picks up a plate that has, written around its rim (in Russian), "Give us this day our daily bread." The sailor turns it in his hands and Eisenstein cuts to a closeup of his face that turns hard with rage. He and his fellow sailors look again at the plate. Cut to his face again, full of anger. He raises the plate over his right shoulder; cut to a closer shot of him raising the plate over his left shoulder; cut to him twisting to the right and lifting the plate in the opposite direction; cut to a sharp closeup of his face; cut back to a shot of him holding the plate high above his right shoulder, bringing it down full force; cut to its smashing on the table; cut to a shot of the sailor's shoulder, his body bent over; finally, a shot of the table with shards of the broken plate (Figure 2.1).

The fragmentation of the action is something akin to cubism in painting, where objects are broken down into multiple perspectives,

30 Revolution!

Figure 2.1 Battleship Potemkin: the shattering of the plate.

a way of seeing a thing from multiple points of view. For Eisenstein, it functions as emphasis, a splintering manic anger that is fueled by proto-revolutionary outrage at the way people are being treated. The breaking of the plate sets the rest of the film in motion, toward a climax in the extraordinary Odessa steps sequence. Before that, a sacrifice is needed. The second part of the film, "Drama on the Deck," constitutes the revolt itself. The Potemkin's captain orders his men to shoot the sailors who have refused to eat the tainted food. He has them covered in tarpaulin, shrouded from their executioners. The remaining sailors call on their brothers not to shoot, but to join them in mutiny. What follows is a frenzied battle onboard the ship, the montage action expressing the confusion and chaos. An officer is thrown overboard, his fall repeated in a time-bending montage. The valiant mutineer, Vakulinchuk, is shot and falls overboard, his death providing a focal point for the uprising as well as a transition to the city of Odessa, where his body is put on display.

The third part of the film, "A Dead Man Calls for Justice," provides for some of the most lyrical images in the film. Fog over the harbor, ships at anchor, the people of Odessa coming to pay tribute to the fallen hero. They come down a long flight of stairs (Eisenstein narrows the frame to emphasize the vertical movement); they swarm over a pier. They gather to mourn and sing about the Revolution. There is a montage of fists being clenched and raised. "Down with Tsarism," they cry. More and more people gather. An anti-Semite appears among them, a man dressed more fancifully than the others, marked as a petit-bourgeois, a small-property owner whose narrow vision of the world was particularly hated by left-wing revolutionaries. "Kill the Jews," he calls out. He laughs at his own smug racism and there is a montage of turning heads as the crowd turns on him and beats him. Anti-Semitism was (and remains) a difficult problem in Russia. Eisenstein, who was Jewish, was particularly sensitive to the issue, and his inclusion of this episode was a brave statement of an ideal—that the revolutionary state would be free of petty bigotry. This section was censored in a 1950 cut of the film made by the Russians.[8]

The sequence continues in a lyrical mood as boats from the shore sail out to greet the sailors of the Potemkin, flying the red flag of revolution. More people gather on the Odessa steps, looking out at and cheering the ship. The formal patterns of the ships and the people are articulated in careful patterns, in montage structures based on dynamic movements and visual elements in the numerous shots. We are introduced to various characters: an elderly nurse dressed in black; a mother and her child; a man with no legs. Eisenstein, in an essay on film language, analyzed this sequence, breaking it down to the very number of boats or people in any given montage cell. Here is an example:

> There is a new quality in this shot, for it is both static and mobile— the mast being vertical and motionless, while the flag flutters in the wind ... But the change from sail to banner translates a principle of plastic unification to an ideological-thematic unification. This is no longer a vertical, a plastic union of separate elements of the composition,—*this is a revolutionary banner, uniting battleship, yawls and shore.*[9]

Every shot and every edit is prepared and analyzed for maximum ideological effect.

"SUDDENLY . . ." a title card announces (Figure 2.2), and there is a quick, asynchronous montage of a woman wildly shaking her head in terror (the head shaking, like the plate breaking, is cut into an atemporal sequence of shots so that she seems to be shaking over and over again). Men and women flee down the steps. A woman with an umbrella heads directly to the camera. In a far shot from behind a statue, we see why: government troops are descending in a line down

32 Revolution!

the steps, firing on the crowd. What follows ratchets up the chaos that Eisenstein portrayed earlier during the scene of revolt on the Potemkin. It is expanded into a violently rhythmic representation of alarm and violence against the people in groups and individually. A legless man uses his arms to flee down the steps. A man falls: we see a closeup of his legs buckling as he falls; there is a cut to another man falling. Is this the falling man's point of view of another man falling? It isn't clear. Eisenstein cuts back to the first shot of the man falling, and then a far shot of his falling over on the steps.

Crowds and individuals. Lines of troops descending, pushing the crowd down the steps. The camera tracks them as they flee. A little boy is shot. The crowd tramples him. His mother picks up his body and moves against the troops, going up the steps as they push downward. She pleads for mercy and is shot. In the midst of this, the elderly woman in black with a white shawl and glasses rises up, urging the crowd to plead for mercy. The woman carrying her child is shot point blank. Cossacks—the dreaded troops on horseback, brandishing swords—join the soldiers in slaughtering the crowd. Then the climactic montage. The followers of the elderly woman in black are shot down. A woman with a baby carriage pauses at the top of the stairs. There are closeups of her and her baby. The soldiers continue

Figure 2.2 "Suddenly."

their inexorable march. She is shot. First we see her contorted face in closeup; the wheels of the baby carriage totter at the edge of the steps; another closeup of the woman in pain; she clutches her waist; the Cossacks are attacking the crowd; the woman clutches her waist, her white gloves are bloodied. In a wider shot, she begins sinking to the ground; a closeup of her face, as she sinks out of the frame; a wider shot of her falling, slightly earlier than we saw her fall in a previous shot. The carriage totters; the soldiers march; she falls again—time is extended. She falls against the carriage. A brief shot of the carnage on the steps and we return to her falling on the carriage, sending it careening down the steps (Figures 2.3 and 2.4).

As the carriage falls, we are shown a closeup of the older woman in black. There are shots of appalled spectators observing the carriage fall; it speeds its fall and begins to tip the baby out; closeups of the Cossacks, cutting people down with their swords. A closeup of the elderly woman in black. Her eye has been shot out (Figure 2.5). This grisly shot is so potent that it inspired the British painter, Francis Bacon, obsessed with wounds and bodies in distress, to recreate her wounded face on canvas.

The conventions of dramatic film, revolutionary or not, must take its narrative to its nadir before there is an upward swing. The politics

Figure 2.3 Soldiers shoot down the woman and her wounded child.

Figure 2.4 The woman and the baby carriage.

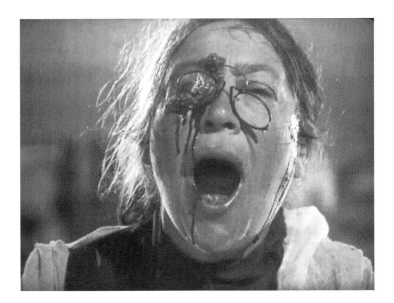

Figure 2.5 The woman shot in the eye.

of drama, melodrama especially, demand an excess of pain, emotional or physical, to be inflicted before there is release. It is the convention of revolutionary film in particular to depict the oppressed in as desperate a situation as possible before they rise up and overthrow their oppressors. We see this happening in the early mutiny sequences of *Battleship Potemkin*. But the way in which Eisenstein has set up the Odessa steps sequence does not allow the people to rise up alone. The forces destroying them are too strong. It takes the victorious revolutionaries on the ship to fire at Odessa and its troops to bring an end to the slaughter. Part 5 of the film, "The Meeting with the Squadron," supplies that victory—after they convince other ships to join them. After the initial firing on the Odessa opera house, whose stone lions appear to rise up with the onslaught, there is a long, languorous sequence as the sailors await the fleet. The sailors of the Potemkin spearhead the Revolution at sea. The squadron declares revolutionary brotherhood with them, and the red flag flies.

We do not see any further action on the steps and can assume the initial firing of the Potemkin's guns stopped the slaughter. But assumption barely matters in Eisenstein's film. What does matter, particularly in revolutionary fiction, is the proclamation of brotherhood, here among the sailors. "Bourgeois" drama celebrates the redemption of individuals and the saving of the captive heroine. Revolutionary fiction demands collective action and the overthrow of the old regime. *Battleship Potemkin* is one semi-fictional presentation of that collective action (Eisenstein went to a larger scope in his history of the Revolution, *October*). Therefore, the final section of the film is taken up with montages of ship machinery, the waiting sailors, and the final joining of the fleet in the battle for liberation. The collective is all.

The liberation of the arts sparked by the Russian Revolution came to an end in the 1930s. Revolution turned to oppression under the rule of Josef Stalin, and experimentation was squelched under the accusation of "formalism." Stalin believed that the avant-garde was too far ahead of the people's ability to understand their work. He wanted his art simple, heroic, and always in praise of the Revolution and himself. The result was a genre known as Soviet Socialist Realism, infamous for its paintings of brave soldiers, farmers and their tractors, and, of course, of Stalin. Another result was the silencing, the humiliating, and sometimes the killing of artists who did not fit the Socialist Realist template. The effect on Sergei Eisenstein was a silencing.

In 1929, his major silent films behind him, he traveled to the U.S. and Mexico, where he shot footage for a film that came to be called *¡Qué viva México!*. This was not Eisenstein's title and not really his film, because he never got to edit it. Nor did he have any more luck in Hollywood, where he pitched an idea to Paramount Pictures for an adaptation of Theodore Dreiser's *An American Tragedy*. Paramount decided they did not want a Communist on their payroll. Eisenstein was recalled to the USSR, where he found himself in Stalin's disfavor. He was able to complete two extraordinary sound films: *Alexander Nevsky* (1938), *Ivan the Terrible*, part I (1945), and, less well known, part II (1958), a film that displeased Stalin and was not released until after both their deaths. During his lifetime, unable to make the films he wanted to, he spent much of his time writing essays about montage theory and corresponding with his American friends and admirers, Charlie Chaplin, Orson Welles, and Walt Disney.

One of the great political filmmakers, who at one time wanted to make Karl Marx's massive work of economic and social theory, *Das Kapital*, into a film, fell victim to totalitarian politics. The films he did make and the large amount of theory he wrote about them represent an acute knowledge of the ways in which the formal properties of a work of art communicate its politics. His films, along with the work of other revolutionary artists, demonstrated how politics and formal construction merged in the ways that political works were made politically. (Films like Woody Allen's *Bananas* (1971) and Brian De Palma's *The Untouchables* (1987) parody the baby carriage sequence from *Battleship Potemkin* without any political force.) Perhaps only the German left-wing playwright Bertolt Brecht was his equal in his depth of understanding of the potency of form. We will talk about Brecht as we go along. We will also have the opportunity to look at other, more contemporary revolutionary films. But first, we need to consider the other end of the political spectrum.

Notes

1 Sergei Eisenstein, "Dickens, Griffith, and the Film Today," *The Film Form: Essays in Film Theory*, trans. Jay Leyda (New York: Harcourt, 1977), 234–235.
2 For the history of the Classical Hollywood Style, see David Bordwell, Janet Staiger, and Kristin Thompson, *The Classical Hollywood Cinema* (New York: Columbia University Press, 1987).
3 Eisenstein, 239.
4 Quoted in Peter Wollen, *Signs and Meaning in the Cinema* (Bloomington, IN: Indiana University Press, 1972), 41.
5 See Dušan Radunović, "The Shifting Protocols of the Visible: The Becoming of Sergei Eisenstein's *The Battleship Potemkin*," *Film History: An International Journal*, vol. 29, no. 2, 2017, pp. 66–90.
6 See www.historytoday.com/richard-cavendish/mutiny-potemkin.

7 "A Dialectical Approach to Film Form," 44.
8 Radunović, 78–79.
9 "Film Language," 119.

Further reading

Sergei Eisenstein, *The Film Sense*, ed. and trans. Jay Leyda (New York: Harcourt Brace Jovanovich, 1975).
—— *The Film Form: Essays in Film Theory*, ed. and trans. Jay Leyda (San Diego, CA: Harcourt Brace Jovanovich, 1977).
Davin Mayer, *Sergei M. Eisenstein's Potemkin: A Shot-by-Shot Presentation* (New York: Grossman, 1972).
Dušan Radunović, "The Shifting Protocols of the Visible: The Becoming of Sergei Eisenstein's *The Battleship Potemkin*," *Film History: An International Journal*, vol. 29, no. 2, 2017, pp. 66–90.

3 Leni Riefenstahl and "Fascinating Fascism"
Triumph of the Will (1935)

Earlier, I spoke about the political spectrum—the continuum from left to right. We examined the extreme left of the spectrum in our discussion of *Battleship Potemkin*, and now we go to the extreme right, and in doing so, I need to clarify some conceptions and misconceptions and to talk about nuance. When we move to the extremities of the political spectrum, to totalitarianism, there tends to be a point of contact. Stalinism and Nazism have commonalities: they are dictatorships with all power concentrated in the hands of brutal leaders, whose task, they believe, is to eliminate any real or perceived opposition to their regime. Much of their policy is based on paranoia. Communism, in theory, and as Marx conceived it, is much less virulent than Stalinism, and is based on an analysis of capitalism and its oppression of the working class. It envisions the revolution to a classless society in which there is no private ownership of the means of production, no private property (the middle class, the bourgeoisie, would disappear)—everything is owned by everyone. An unrealistic ideal, as is its notion of a selfless sharing of society's wealth. Marxist Communism has never quite worked out in practice; its ideal of a communal, classless society is impractical in the world of realpolitik and the very human propensity to rule or be ruled and to be free to own things.

Fascism works in the opposite direction. At the outset, it concentrates power in the hands of a strong leader and sets up a corporate state in which business and government work hand in hand. It is strongly, obsessively nationalist, proclaiming the state as the most important entity, often looking back at an imagined golden age when the country was great, a time it aspires to recreate. Fascism bases its ideological strength on the opposition to minority groups: Communists and Jews in its earlier incarnations; Middle-Eastern immigrants in its current form. Fascism pretends a populist stance, against "elites" and for working people; it uses populism as a screen to diffuse its gathering of power around an elite group, headed by the leader—the Führer in Germany or Il Duce in Italy.

Il Duce, Benito Mussolini, started the fascist movement in Italy in 1922 (he took the name from the Latin *fasci*, the image of an axe bound in the middle of rods or sheaves of wheat). Beginning as a socialist, Mussolini discovered that the contemporary weakness of the state was ripe for a strongman and his "black shirts" to take over to save the country from Communists and other imagined threats against his notion of order. He ruled until Italy's defeat in WWII when the people turned on him, shot him and his wife, and hung them up by their heels in the town square. We will discuss Italian Fascism in more detail when we look at Bernardo Bertolucci's *The Conformist* in Chapter 8.

Fascism spread to Spain in the 1930s when, in 1936, General Francisco Franco led a right-wing revolt against the established government. The civil war that ensued divided not only the country, but the world as well; European fascists fought on the side of Franco's forces, the Nationalists; Leftists, including the United States' Abraham Lincoln brigade, fought on the side of the Loyalists. Ernest Hemingway covered the civil war and wrote his novel *For Whom the Bell Tolls* based on his experience. Pablo Picasso painted his huge, terrifying mural *Guernica* about the horrors of that conflagration. Franco's forces won the civil war, and he remained as Spain's dictator until his death in 1975, his longevity becoming a long-running joke on *Saturday Night Live*.

The most virulent form of Fascism by far occurred in Germany. National Socialism, better known as Nazism, grew out of a history of Germanic romanticism, nationalism, and racism, hatred of Jews, belief in racial superiority, and mystical attachment to "blood and soil." But the immediate causes of Nazism were Germany's humiliating defeat in WWI and the crushing reparations the victorious powers leveled against the country. The worldwide recession of 1929 hit Germany very hard, and political turmoil that came from all parts of spectrum, but especially the left, allowed the country, and its business leaders in particular, to be ready for a strongman. They found one in the failed Austrian painter, Adolf Hitler. Hitler's and the Nazis' rise to power is a complicated and violent affair, and much has been written about it. What is important to note is that Hitler did not come to power with a coup or a revolution. (He did try a coup in 1923, and wound up in jail, where he wrote his book, his defense of anti-Semitism, *Mein Kampf*— "My Struggle.") His party was elected to Germany's parliament, the Reichstag, and he was appointed Chancellor in 1933. Once there, he coalesced his power through intimidation, beatings, and killings, and initiated the most violent and destructive regime of the 20th century.

Hitler's enemies of choice were Communists and Jews. His method of dealing with them—Jews in particular—was to demonize them and then kill them. It seems, from the distance of time, almost like a horrible work of fiction, the rounding up and gassing to death of millions of people, and, in fact, the Nazis wanted it to appear like a fiction. Their theory of "the big lie" was to create events, like "the final solution"—the extermination of the Jews—so outrageous, so unbelievable that they would not be believed. But the genocide was very real and believable (though not by the West at the time). Once we are able to understand the depths of depravity to which a civilized culture can sink, once we see the images of the camps, we can begin to understand the reality of what happened a relatively short time ago.

Or can we? Will we ever understand the "why"? The Auschwitz survivor and writer Primo Levi told a story about when, as a young prisoner, he reached for an icicle to quench his thirst. The prison guard knocked it from his hand. "Why?" Levi asked. "There is no why here," answered the guard.[1] Nazism was a politics of rational irrationality. They reasoned well what they were doing; they kept meticulous records of their human exterminations; they used the tools of modern warfare; they developed television and guided missiles. Were it not for the USSR and the Allied forces, they might well have taken over Europe and Russia. By the time the war ended, they had murdered six million Jews. Those imprisoned and murdered did not know why; the Nazis did. They needed an ethnic scapegoat to feed their lust for blood and power.

Joseph Goebbels was the Nazi's Minister of Public Enlightenment and Propaganda, a major position for a regime that used all means to let their own people and the world at large know how wonderful and how terrifying they were. But Goebbels had a rival, a former dancer, movie actress, and director, an intimate friend of the Führer, a person who would become the most powerful woman in the regime: Leni Riefenstahl.

Riefenstahl came to prominence in a series of "mountain films" that celebrated strenuous activity in mystical landscapes, a connection with "blood and soil" that was so much a foundation of Nazi mythology and ideology. In 1932, she directed and played in *The Blue Light*. She is an Italian peasant, Junta, the only person who can scale the perilous mountain heights to gather the mysterious glowing crystals at the peak. But when the greedy townspeople learn how to climb the mountain themselves, they despoil the site of its mystical treasures. In her grief, Junta falls from the peak to her death. In its simplicity and, at times, visual lyricism, the film appealed to Hitler's dreams of strenuous endeavor and sacrifice, of death as the noblest achievement of the Germanic hero. (Nazism was a death cult.)

Riefenstahl and Hitler became friends. She slept in his room, but apparently not with him.[2] Hitler asked her to make a film, *Victory of Faith*, a documentary of the 1933 Nuremburg rally. The film was lost for years, perhaps because, in addition to Hitler, it celebrated the SA (Sturmabteilung), a military group of murderers under the leadership of Ernst Röhm, a rival to Hitler's power. Hitler had Röhm and most of his followers killed in "the night of the long knives," and Riefenstahl's film disappeared until a copy was discovered in the early 1990s. It is something of a ragged affair, carelessly edited, full of people raising their arms in the Nazi salute. Only in the scenes of mass rallies can we detect what was to come, the film that would be the lasting document of Nazi propaganda and Leni Riefenstahl's infamy: *Triumph of the Will*.

Triumph of the Will is a documentary of a Nazi rally held in Nuremburg in 1934. But calling it a "documentary" stretches the term a bit. We usually think of a documentary as a film that observes events and listens to individuals who talk off the cuff about what they know or think about the film's topic. *Triumph* is no such thing. The rally was, in part, staged for Riefenstahl to film it. "Commissioned by order of the Führer," reads the opening title. Towers were set up for her cameras to achieve dramatic crane shots; multiple camerapersons were allowed to film throughout the crowd and the ceremonies. And ceremony it is. *Triumph of the Will* is about a tribal gathering celebrating a ceremony of worship for their leader, who, at the beginning of the film, descends in his plane from the heavens.

Even from this god's-eye view, masses of people can be seen marching in perfectly ordered columns. On landing, masses of people offer the Nazi salute. Masses of people constitute the key reference of this film. Riefenstahl's method is to overwhelm the viewer with crowd-packed images, to, in effect, punish the viewer with the repetition of adoring people, stern, speechmaking Nazi officials, massed troops, a fanaticism of order, adoration, and submission. I use the word "punish" with care. For contemporary viewers—you and I—watching *Triumph of the Will* is punishingly boring; its main attraction is a kind of amazed response to the power it must have had on its contemporary German audience. Therefore, it is necessary to enter the film as if it were a time capsule, revealing a society gone mad not in a chaotic manner (the chaos was in the depression-wracked years that led up to Hitler), but in an obsessively ordered, vicious state of like-minded German citizens, ranked in their response to a psychotic, charismatic leader.

42 Leni Riefenstahl and "Fascinating Fascism"

The narrative of the film is jagged in its attempt to follow the chronology of the rally. Hitler descends. At night, in front of his hotel, there are rallies. Torches burn in the dark. In the morning, windows open and Nazi flags are unfurled. There is a languid sequence in which the camera views the city while floating down its river. And then a dissolve from a low-angle shot moving around the spires of a cathedral to aerial shots of masses of tents in orderly rows. The Hitler Youth, camping out. Young boys come pouring out of their tents. Shirtless, they blow trumpets and beat on huge drums hanging from their necks. We see them dress and shave, combing one another's hair, scrubbing one another's backs. They prepare breakfast in huge boiling vats. Everything is slightly larger than life. Later in the film, Riefenstahl focuses on an unnervingly intense boy beating his drum, introducing the Hitler Youth once again, this time in perfectly ordered masses, addressed by the Führer (Figure 3.1).

The male homosocial bond is an important part of Nazi ideology. These (mostly) blond boys and young men frolicking, wrestling, and banging drums represent the Aryan ideal of the future of the race. Their physical intimacy tends to blend them into a happy promise of the new regime—vital, energetic, optimistic. They tell a sympathetic viewer that the continuity of the patriarchal order, of the race itself, is being generated before his eyes. There is some room for women

Figure 3.1 The intensity of dedication: the drummer boy in *Triumph of the Will*.

(the main purpose of women under Nazism was to breed more Nazis). The following sequence features a march of women, and a few men, in local, peasant costumes, celebrating the various states that make up the German Reich. Hitler shakes their hands and they look on in awe.

And then begin the speeches. Many Nazi officials and dignitaries give speeches throughout the film, climaxing in a long harangue by Hitler himself. The speakers are photographed in closeup or from a low angle, praising the Führer and the new regime. Though one does growl, "A people which does not hold with the purity of its race will perish," Riefenstahl is quite circumspect in editing out any overt anti-Semitism. She wants instead to present a chorus of adulation and enthusiasm, an infectious drumbeat of praise for the Reich and its leader.

As the film proceeds, so does Riefenstahl's emphasis on the obsessive order of the various groups in attendance by means of the way she stages and photographs them. She will often use a telephoto lens to compress space, making the crowds appear even denser. The climactic sequence occurs just past the halfway mark of the film as Hitler, along with his chief assassin, Heinrich Himmler, and another official, enter the stadium to honor the Nazi dead (Figure 3.2). Riefenstahl begins with her camera high above the scene. The three figures walk alone along a broad avenue flanked on each side by enormous rectangles of massed onlookers, appearing as if they were carefully trimmed formal gardens of humanity. She then cuts to the opposite side, behind pillars. The angle is just about eye level and we see the three figures approaching while far behind them are hanging three enormous vertical Nazi flags. The camera tracks to the left. The next cut is a high-angle shot of the three figures approaching the site where they will go through the ceremony. There are more marches through the arena marked by a dramatic rising crane shot moving high above the massed crowds. (You can see the elevator that was built for Riefenstahl's camera attached to one of the poles holding a Nazi flag.)

The latter half of the film is filled with a variety of marches, images of the Führer, and masses of people. It all ends with a speech by Hitler, a guttural, melodramatic, self-satisfied call to unity, with many "sieg heils" from the audience. Rudolf Hess, one of Hitler's henchmen, ends the proceedings: "The Party is Hitler! But Hitler is Germany as Germany is Hitler!" The film concludes with the crowd singing the Horst Wessel song—the party's anthem (written by a former pimp)— more marchers, and dissolved over all, a giant Swastika.

This is all more than spectacle: it becomes something like an abstract patterning of the geometric formation of bodies and their obeisance to their leader—two essential qualities of Fascism. And Fascism, Nazism

Figure 3.2 March through the stadium (*Triumph of the Will*).

in particular, articulates its politics by a kind of willing mass hypnosis of the people, who, unhappy with their lives and their country's condition, give themselves over to their most worshipful, most racist, most violent instincts. *Giving over.* Fascism is founded, as I noted, on a carefully planned irrationality, focused on a group of people to hate—Jews in Hitler's case. Irrationality can be orchestrated by means of spectacle, channeled narrowly by being lost in the immensity and submission of the faithful. Yielding individuality, believing in national and racial superiority, worshipping a leader, singling out a racial minority to oppress or even destroy—these are all signs of a cultural, political, and ideological sickness. For reason and the embrace of difference, they substitute rage and hatred.

The essayist and filmmaker Susan Sontag analyzed fascist aesthetics in her 1975 essay about Leni Riefenstahl, "Fascinating Fascism." It is worth quoting at length:

> Fascist aesthetics . . . flow from (and justify) a preoccupation with situations of control, submissive behavior, and extravagant effort; they exalt two seemingly opposite states, egomania and servitude. The relations of domination and enslavement take the form of a characteristic pageantry: the massing of groups of people;

the turning of people into things; the multiplication of things and grouping of people/things around an all-powerful, hypnotic leader figure or force. The fascist dramaturgy centers on the orgiastic transactions between mighty forces and their puppets. Its choreography alternates between ceaseless motion and a congealed, static, "virile" posing. Fascist art glorifies surrender; it exalts mindlessness: it glamorizes death.[3]

Triumph of the Will is a drama of mighty forces and their puppets. It trades in mass adoration and hyper-orderly obeisance. The film hides its glamorizing of death under its numbing exaltation of mindlessness. To admire, indeed worship, Hitler and Nazism is to lose individuality and reason. *Triumph* assures the sympathetic viewer—perhaps even hypnotizes him—that this is the appropriate response to Hitler and his Reich.

Leni Riefenstahl made one other film for the Nazis, a big, two-part documentary of the 1936 Berlin Olympics, *Olympia*, released in 1938. A glorification of the body and of Hitler, the film contains some fine moments. It does not shrink from showing the victorious African-American athlete, Jesse Owens, and its final sequence of divers is shot in slow motion and edited in a way that gives the illusion of an ecstatic aerial ballet. But it is in its very adoration of the body that the film exposes its fascist aesthetics. The ecstatic quality of some of its scenes betrays an obsessive choreography of ceaseless motion and a congealed, static, "virile" posing.

And then there was WWII. Riefenstahl managed to get herself to the Polish front, where she witnessed the slaughter of Jews and showed some genuine horror. As one of her biographers says, photographs of her at the time "reveal a moment of truth in Riefenstahl's life, her world breaking apart as reality descended on her . . . No one was paying any attention to her command, and there would be no lovely images for her to exploit."[4] It was only a moment. Before the war ended, she began work on what would be her last film, another mountain melodrama, *Lowlands*. She plundered Gypsy concentration camps (Gypsies were another group the Nazis regarded as subhuman) for extras. Many of them, including children, were sent to extermination camps after the shoot.

After the war, she was briefly imprisoned by the Americans and then by the French. She was acquitted of war crimes and went on to finish her film, becoming a photographer of, most notably, an obscure African tribe, the Nuba, and she also photographed celebrities like Mick Jagger. She became a celebrity herself, who, to her dying day, insisted that she knew nothing about Nazi atrocities and had no close connection to the Nazi high command. She died in 2003 at age 101.

Triumph of the Will has had a long afterlife. Frank Capra, whose films we will discuss in the next chapter, used clips from it in his WWII anti-Nazi propaganda films. George Lucas copied the scene of the three figures marching down the center aisle with troops massed on either side for the end of his first *Star Wars* (1977). Fascism has had an afterlife as well, as a subject for filmmakers, as we will see in Chapter 8. Far-right-wing movements are alive in Western Europe, nationalism and populism have overtaken U.S. politics, anti-Semitism is never absent, and Muslims have become a new target for hate. Perhaps there will never again be Nazi rallies as spectacular as that created for *Triumph of the Will*, though images of massed admirers and troops are a staple of Chinese and North Korean newsreels. A rally on the grounds of the University of Virginia in 2017 featured a large gang of men with Tiki torches yelling anti-Semitic slogans. The film, as tedious as it may be to watch today, remains an important reminder of a fanaticism that took hold of an entire people and led to the near extermination of another. It may be a template for the rise of neo-fascism today.

The film also continues the argument about art and politics. Is it possible to consider *Triumph of the Will* as a work of art? Are propaganda and art irreconcilable? We noted that despite its repellent content, *The Birth of a Nation* is an important milestone in the development of cinema. Riefenstahl's film is a milestone in the making of the propaganda film, but like Griffith's, it promotes the indefensible. Still, it remains a part of the cinematic memory; a reminder, if we need one. *Birth* memorializes the racist roots of American history. *Triumph* helps us remember the savagery of the mid-20th century. Without their images, our memory would be poorer, and we would forget not only the horrors of the past but the power of images to evoke them.

Notes

1 Primo Levi, *Survival in Auschwitz: The Nazi Assault on Humanity*, trans. Stuart Woolf (New York: Touchstone, 1996), 29.
2 See Karen Wieland, *Dietrich & Riefenstahl: Hollywood, Berlin, and a Century of Two Lives*, trans. Shelley Frisch (New York: Liveright, 2011), 146.
3 *The New York Review of Books* (February 6, 1975), www.nybooks.com/articles/1975/02/06/fascinating-fascism.
4 Wieland, *Dietrich & Riefenstahl*, 326, 338.

Further reading

Steven Bach, *Leni: The Life and Work of Leni Riefenstahl* (New York: Alfred A. Knopf, 2007).

William Shirer, *The Rise and Fall of the Third Reich: A History of Nazi Germany* (New York: Simon & Schuster, 1959, 2011).

Jürgen Trimborn, *Leni Riefenstahl: A Life* (Faber & Faber, Inc., 2002, translated by Edna McCown in 2007).

4 American democracy and Frank Capra
Mr. Smith Goes to Washington (1939)

The 1930s were a decade of political turmoil across the globe. German Nazis and Italian Fascists took over much of Europe and Northern Africa. Late in the decade, Great Britain suffered massive bombing by the Germans. The United States was suffering under a massive economic depression. Millions of people were out of work and there were breadlines as the hungry sought relief. Strong voices from the right and the left tried to gain the attention and allegiance of a beaten population. Anti-Semitism thrived; anti-black prejudice and violence continued.

Franklin Delano Roosevelt was elected President in 1933, the same year that Hitler took power in Germany. Roosevelt was an activist, a slightly left-of-center Democrat, who believed strongly in government and its role in supporting everything from labor to the arts. He attempted to conquer the Depression (and save capitalism) by creating government jobs across the board and pushing the leftward boundaries of liberal democracy (and struggling against right-wing opposition) to get his programs enacted. He supported the arts and underwrote works of the imagination through such programs as the Federal Theatre Project. He strengthened labor laws and offered aid to farmers; he placed some curbs on business abuses; and, perhaps his greatest legacy, he created social security. These policies worked up to a point because the Depression did not come to an end until the U.S. entered WWII in 1941. Wartime industrial production set the economy back in motion.

American film was deeply involved and reactive both to the Depression and to FDR and his "New Deal." Warner Bros. in particular produced a number of films that confronted the ordeal of the disenfranchised and beaten. *Wild Boys of the Road* (William A. Wellman, 1933) depicted displaced young people, rootless, homeless, at the mercy of an unfriendly, unwelcoming social environment. *I Am a Fugitive from a Chain Gang* (Mervyn LeRoy, 1932) is one of the darkest films to come out of the Depression, an indictment of the cruelty of southern prisons and the reducing of a man of means and talent into becoming a thief. Warner Bros. also produced musicals, dark ones about the Depression and the attempt to sing and dance our way out of the gloom. "We're in the money, we're in the money / We've got a lot of what it takes to get along! / We're in the money, that sky is sunny, / Old Man Depression you are through, you done us wrong . . ." So went the hopeful song-and-dance number, with singers dressed in gold coins, in the Busby Berkeley number in the film *Gold Diggers of 1933* (Mervyn LeRoy, 1933).

Other studios and other filmmakers faced the Depression with different styles and different politics. The most famous was Frank Capra, whose populist films of the 1930s traced the Depression from the run on the banks in *American Madness* (1932) to the growth of a native fascism in *Meet John Doe* (1941). We spoke about populism in regard to D. W. Griffith, and I noted that his short film, *Corner in Wheat*, is "populism writ small." It is the opposite in Capra's films, where populism is writ with a large, broad brush. For Capra, to put it in the simplest terms, there are two classes of people: rich plutocrats, who own the most money and property and want more, and the "little guy," of modest means, trying to live a "normal," even carefree life, and who is threatened by the plutocrat's rapacious greed. Sometimes, Capra will play his populism for laughs, as in his screwball comedy, *It Happened One Night* (1934). Here an heiress, escaping from her rich father, goes on the road with a "regular guy," a newspaper reporter, resulting in humorous encounters and a final, sexual union. Given the power of the Production Code—the office set up by the studios to censor filmmakers' work—the sexual tension between the couple is displaced, symbolized by the curtain they set up between their motel room beds. "The wall of Jericho," they call it, which comes tumbling down at film's end.

As always in Capra's films, it's the "little guy" who wins out, but not without considerable suspense as to how this winning might occur. It sometimes appears, as in *Meet John Doe*, where the suicide of the main character appears all but inevitable until the last moment, and especially in *Mr. Smith Goes to Washington*, that Capra and his writers are unsure about how to end their films. No matter how great his faith in the goodness of poor or lower-middle-class people, he is not quite sure that they will prevail in the face of the ugliness that confronts and threatens them. The politics of despair hangs over and under Capra's films, never more obvious than in his postwar 1946 film, *It's a Wonderful Life*, a commercial failure when it first appeared, but now a favorite Christmas movie. James Stewart's George Bailey is a depressed character, trapped in his small town, unable to realize his dreams of world travel. What's more, his father's bank is at risk of being taken over by the town's millionaire, Mr. Potter. About to commit suicide, an angel appears to George to show him the dark, corrupt, violent town of Bedford Falls that would emerge in George's absence. In short, there is no real choice for George Bailey. He must give up his dreams and remain to save his town, its bank, his family. He of course does all of this, with the help of the townspeople, who chip in money to save the bank. In the populist imagination, the politics of despair must ultimately yield to the politics of salvation (and a savior), real or imagined.

I'm using "politics" a bit loosely here. The more appropriate word might be "negotiation," a tension between the power of money and the power of hope. Capra negotiates the terms of who will win and how, often discovering that he has to cheat through the creation of a last-minute rescue so that the struggling protagonist will prevail over the evils of the moneyed elite. But he must also negotiate the shoals of reality, where class differences and the power of money tend to hold permanent sway. When he confronts politics in the specific sense of making laws and getting votes, reality comes extremely close and almost kills the deal, as we will see in *Mr. Smith Goes to Washington*.

But Capra has another deal to make, another kind or degree of politics—the politics of form. Capra was a master of the Classical Hollywood Style, able to build a cinematic world in which incident, character, and the viewer's gaze at the screen are tightly, expertly knit. The negotiation here is more of a guarantee: that his film will entertain, will make you angry at the avaricious rich, will make you cheer for the "little guy," all the while not noticing the expert shot setup and editing that makes all this work so smoothly. Capra's formal mastery creates an apparently seamless story. But there is a nice contradiction: the story, as we'll see, is not seamless. It is ruptured by violence and the immediate impression that its central character will lose to the forces of evil greed and political corruption. In *Mr. Smith*, Capra tries to create a character of pristine innocence (played by James Stewart), and takes him out of a small town which should be his Garden of Eden, but is in fact a snake pit. Capra moves him to the cynical world of Washington politics, where he is almost swallowed whole, almost defeated in his bid to get land for his Boy Rangers, land owned by the terrible political boss Jim Taylor (played by Edward Arnold, one of Capra's favorite heavies), who owns Senator Paine (Claude Raines), Jefferson Smith's mentor.

Seamless storytelling, ruptured story, innocence lost. In someone else's hands, the film could well be a melodrama of the destruction of an innocent man and an indictment of the American political system. But Capra's populism disallows darkness to prevail, even if it means a too sudden reversal of events in the last few minutes of the film. Instead, Capra presents a mix of comedy and melodrama, a potential love interest, a heavy dose of patriotism, and a talent for triangulating the viewer in such a way that her gaze is continually caught by Jefferson Smith's eye on the events he can barely manage.

The opening sequences of the film are entirely under Capra's control and set forth the arc of the film's narrative, thematics, and politics. A senator has died. The current sitting senator, Paine, and boss Taylor, accept Jefferson Smith as a safe, naïve, compliant place-filler so that they can consummate a land deal. At the dinner to celebrate his appointment, Smith's Boy Rangers march and present him with a briefcase. The scene is played for sentimentality and a nicely simulated good will and discomfort. Jeff is embarrassed while Taylor and his aide Chick (the wonderful comic actor Eugene Pallette) pass knowing looks between them. Jeff reminds Paine that he was once friends with Jeff's late father and, on the train to D.C., the two reminisce about the days of commitment to a cause. We have, up to this point, been privy to the underhanded methods that the people who are Jeff's antagonists have used in his appointment. Arriving in Washington, the tone changes twice—to comedy, as Jeff hands Chick the cages of carrier pigeons he has brought with him to bring messages to his mother, and then to patriotic sentimentality as Jeff slips away from his handlers and takes a tour of Washington's monuments.

The tour is done by means of a montage. Not of the Eisenstein variety, but created by a man named Slavko Vorkapich, who adapted some of Eisenstein's techniques for a number of films during the 1930s. Here, accompanied by rousing patriotic music, Jeff excitedly, reverentially, looks at the monuments as they come drifting by his eyes and consciousness. He drives past the Whitehouse and the Capitol, he visits the National Gallery, and he looks at the Constitution. Its words flash across the screen as a giant liberty bell swings into view (yes, the Liberty Bell is in Philadelphia, but the montage is interested in emotional not geographical precision). Jeff stares up at the Washington Monument and as the National Anthem swells, a sculpture of an eagle and a giant American flag dissolve into view. The tour ends at the Lincoln Memorial and the tone turns somber as Smith and others, including a child reading Lincoln's words, and an elderly African-American man, gaze reverentially. "The Red River Valley" swells on the soundtrack. The Liberty Bell rings (Figure 4.1).

Figure 4.1 Reverence at the Lincoln Memorial in *Mr. Smith Goes to Washington*.

This is the kind of sequence that earned Capra's films the somewhat condescending term "Capracorn." There is no question that the montage is overdone, overly sentimental, brimming with a most easily unearned patriotism. But within the context of the film Capra is trying to construct, it is important. Jefferson Smith is about to go up against the political machine (Figure 4.2) and Capra wants to arm both him and the viewer with a sense of innocent righteousness, to, in effect, lay out the patriotic ground on which the ensuing battle will be fought. It is a losing battle from the beginning and to almost the bitter end.

Jefferson Smith is the perfect naïf; journalists paint him as a fool, he fumbles his hat (Capra makes much of this) when he meets Senator Paine's beautiful daughter, he knows nothing about the democratic process. Which, he soon learns, is something less than democratic. He is, in a word, helpless, almost willingly so, and Capra has to give him help, which appears in the form of Saunders (Jean Arthur), Senator Paine's assistant. She and her journalist colleague Diz (Thomas Mitchell), an alcoholic, start out by sharing everyone else's cynicism, but Saunders decides to take Jeff under her care. She is given a misty closeup when Jeff waxes poetic over the bill he wants to introduce. He is impressed by her: "For a woman, you've done awfully well," he tells her.

American democracy and Frank Capra   53

Figure 4.2 Boss Taylor (Edward Arnold) threatens Jeff Smith.

While much is made of the potential sexual attraction between the two, she essentially mothers Jeff into growing up. But growing up into what? His Senate colleagues think he is a fool and when his plan to build a boy's camp on the land boss Taylor and his stooge Senator Paine are counting on owning, he becomes a patsy in an escalating war to destroy him. This is the grimness that underlies the sentimentality of the film. So grim that children's lives are threatened by Taylor's thugs.

This is dramatic enough, but Capra needs to ratchet up the drama within the political framework he establishes from the start. As part of his attempt to remove Jeff, Taylor has Senator Paine create a Senate committee to attempt to impeach Jeff for corruption, complete with forged papers. Despondent, Jeff makes a visit to the Lincoln Memorial and plans to leave town. In the shadows of the monument, Saunders comes to him and, in a very long take (the camera gazes at them without cutting), convinces him to stay and fight (Figure 4.3). Capra then does something interesting. Rather than create an expository scene in which Saunders and Jeff figure out what to do, he cuts immediately to the Senate floor, where Jeff makes an unexpected appearance and commences a filibuster. Capra makes this the dramatic highpoint of the film, creating a sense of hysteria as Jeff, under Saunders' direction,

Figure 4.3 A moment of doubt: Jeff (Jimmy Stewart) and Saunders (Jean Arthur) in the shadows of the Lincoln Memorial.

holds the floor until the Senate agrees to vote on his bill. Capra brings in a real-life newscaster of the time, who explains what a filibuster is and tells us "the galleries are packed. In the diplomatic gallery are the envoys of two dictator powers. They have come here to see what they can't see at home: Democracy in action."

A lesson in legislature procedure and current events; a fight against a corrupt political machine; suspense generated by concern over just how long Jefferson Smith can hold out; revulsion at the strong-arm tactics used by Taylor to destroy Jeff; some comfort taken by the care demonstrated by the leader of the Senate, his judgments and kindly demeanor acting as a surrogate for our own anxious gaze; pleasure at the love blooming between Jeff and Saunders. It is a remarkable balancing act of stimulus and response, and Capra almost fails to bring it off. With two minutes left until the end of the film, Jeff seems licked (Figure 4.4). Hoarse and broken, he passes out amidst the piles of fake letters sent by the Taylor machine to discredit him. Suddenly his patron, the former friend of his father, the creature of the Taylor machine, Senator Paine rushes out, tries to shoot himself, rushes back into the chamber and proclaims his guilt. The place erupts, the young Senate pages jump

American democracy and Frank Capra   55

Figure 4.4 At his wit's end during his filibuster, Jeff tosses the telegrams demanding he give up. Senator Paine (just glimpsed in the left background) will soon break down and admit his complicity.

up and down, Saunders and Diz jump up and down. The Senate leader sits back and, like us, enjoys the show. Fade to black.

Fade up on an audience perhaps not quite convinced that it can be all that easy, or even that Capra believes in democracy as much as the film seems to claim. The fact is that it's not democracy that saves Jefferson Smith and the brutal tactics of Jim Taylor. The only thing that saves his ruin is the last-minute burst of conscience and attempted suicide of his mentor. In other words, it isn't the work of a self-correcting political system, bringing justice to the helpless, but the actions of an individual driven by his own demons. We could look at this as the politics of personal redemption and see Jefferson Smith as the moral center of the film. But if we do (and I think Capra sees it this way), then the film has undermined itself. It is not about democracy in action but individuals divided into caricatures of good and evil, of evil becoming good, of innocence and, of course, love triumphant. This makes *Mr. Smith Goes to Washington* little different than any other film, except that it dresses itself in the trappings of Washington politics.

Capra's heart, if not his head, was in the right place. Sentimentalizing politics was one way to get a film made about politics at all. At the same time, it taps into a particular American response to politics: that it is a joke. While, as a culture, we tend to believe, or hope, that the next President or Congress person we elect will change things, we also know, on some level, that this won't happen, that they are all frauds or corrupt. This cynicism mixed with hope and a measure of despair keeps driving us somewhat blindly, which is precisely what happens in *Mr. Smith*. Sentimentality serves as a cushion against the blows of cynicism.

The decade of *Mr. Smith Goes to Washington* was a difficult time, economically, culturally, politically. The only cushion in the day-to-day world (as opposed to the world of movies) was Franklin Delano Roosevelt, whose persona and presidency offered real hope and some success to those suffering from the Great Depression. And then came WWII. As I noted earlier, the ramp up of wartime production was a deciding factor in banishing the Depression. But not depression, at least on a cultural level. Of course, the country rallied behind the war effort after the bombing of Pearl Harbor on December 7, 1941, and Hollywood followed suit, producing war films as well as films about the courage of those who remained at home. The U.S. government opened an office to keep watch over film production, especially war films, to be sure they put our soldiers and their cause in the best light. After years of working to keep the government out of censoring their productions, the studios had to bow to the politics of wartime.

Frank Capra did his part. He received a commission as Major in the Army Signal Corps, and was eventually promoted to Colonel. Most importantly, he produced, for the War Department, the *Why We Fight* series of propaganda films made to explain the war to the soldiers who fought it and to the American public. Under Capra's supervision a variety of Hollywood talent created these short, dramatic, rhythmically compelling documentaries. They made use of mostly found and some staged footage, of maps animated by the Walt Disney studio, of rapid montage. The first film of the series, *Prelude to War*, begins with a montage of battle footage and goes on to explain a divided world: free (the U.S.) and slaves (Europe and Asia under Nazi and Japanese control). Light and dark. Black and white. The images (some taken from *Triumph of the Will*) and descriptions are stark, stereotyped (racist where the Japanese are concerned), simplified, and unrelenting. In propaganda, simplification is necessary and, without the formal subtlety and adventurousness of Sergei Eisenstein, the films seem a bit bombastic to us today. But we need to remember that the United States before Pearl Harbor was isolationist and wanted no part of "foreign entanglements" after WWI—*Prelude to War* addresses this—and Pearl Harbor may have changed minds but not hearts. It was the job of Capra and his team to convince the soldiers and citizens about the unquestioning necessity of combat.

The light and the dark. It's a theme Capra carries over to his first postwar feature, *It's a Wonderful Life*. I noted earlier that this film hinges on James Stewart's George Bailey being given a vision of what his town would be without him: a dark, violent place. This vision would not have been unusual to a contemporary audience, because darkness had settled over much of Hollywood's output. In retrospect, it has been called film noir. At the time, it was a sign of a despairing public mood, captured in films full of shadows and pain, violence and murderous women. Noir began just as the war was ending and continued through the early 1950s; it foreshadows and then shadows the politics of fear that marked the postwar period. We will return to this in Chapter 9.

Hollywood no longer does "Capracorn." Perhaps audiences are too sophisticated for the big sentimentality that Capra's films generate. But there is no dearth of films about men (and sometimes women) going after big business or big government, rooting out corruption. In *Miss Sloane* (John Madden, 2016), a liberal lobbyist, played by Jessica Chastain, takes on the gun lobby and fights for an amendment that would require background checks. Unlike Capra's heroes, she is a flawed character who takes sleeping pills and hires a male prostitute because she doesn't have time for dating. But she fights nonetheless, confronting a corrupt Senator and endangering her own career (she winds up doing jail time). Like Jefferson Smith, she fights against almost insuperable odds. Unlike Jeff, she gets little assistance in her struggle. In front of a Senate hearing, her male escort denies knowing her, thereby saving her reputation. Thanks to clever technology, she gets the goods on the corrupt Senator. But overall, and despite an obligatory upbeat ending, the film shows even less optimism than Capra did some fifty years earlier. Politics on the electoral level haven't changed all that much; our attitudes toward them have. We tend to take for granted that corruption and powerlessness are a given. Populism uses cynicism as fuel.

Further reading

Frank Capra, *The Name Above the Title: An Autobiography* (New York: Da Capo Press, 1997).

Mark Harris, *Five Came Back: A Story of Hollywood and the Second World War* (New York: Penguin Random House, 2015).

Joseph McBride, *Frank Capra: The Catastrophe of Success* (New York: Simon and Schuster, 1992).

Jeffery Richards, "Frank Capra and the Cinema of Populism" in Bill Nichols, ed., *Movies and Methods*, Vol. 1 (Berkeley and Los Angeles, CA: University of California Press, 1976), 65–77.

Robert Sklar and Vito Zagarrio, eds., *Frank Capra: Authorship and the Studio System* (Philadelphia, PA: Temple University Press, 1998).

5 Revolution in the 1960s
The Battle of Algiers (1966)

In this chapter, we make a long leap, from an American populist film of the 1930s to an Italian-Algerian film made in the late 1960s about the Algerian Revolution that took place in the 1950s and early 60s. *Mr. Smith Goes to Washington* is a film about the recapturing of the status quo, the reestablishment of American democracy, and the end of corruption. It is a film full of American pessimism and optimism: the certainty that things are not well and the hope they can get better. The film focuses on the individual qualities of innocence lost and found. The film we discuss here is not about innocence or even individual behavior; neither is it about a return to an ideal of the normal. It is about upheaval, revolution, the overthrow of the ruling regime, and, in a more global sense, an attack on colonialism, which is where we begin.

There are two methods of owning people. Slavery is constituted by a one-to-one ownership of master and slave. In the pre-Civil War South one owner might have had many enslaved people and in many slave states ownership of enslaved people was a given among that class of whites who could afford to keep people as property. Still, slavery was a personal matter, something slave owners held as a matter of pride, even of natural right. Then there is colonialism, in which one country figuratively, economically, and administratively owns one or more other countries. This may not constitute slavery in the literal sense. Colonized peoples are ostensibly free to carry on their lives under the rules set down by the ruling country. But they are looked down upon and regimented by people and laws foreign to them. Their customs become spectacle for the colonizers; their aspirations to self-government often brutally repressed. Colonization occurs because the ruling country wants simply to exercise power or wants the natural resources of the colonized country. In the case of England's colonization of India in the mid-18th century, Britain wanted both. They waged war against the people on the subcontinent, introduced laws, created complex bureaucracies, attempted to impose Christianity on Hindus and Muslims, and built railroads to speed the movement of exports. They took the goods they wanted and remained in India for over a century. By the mid-1940s, the country became less necessary to the British economy and nationalist movements in India itself led to independence.[1]

The story of South Africa is somewhat different and even grimmer. The colonizers, first the Dutch and then the English, created a white minority population and culture, bent on keeping the African majority at arm's length. To this end, they created Apartheid, which kept the native black population segregated in deplorable conditions. Apartheid was a nasty combination of colonization and slavery, broken again by a nationalist movement spearheaded by many brave left-of-center South Africans, some at the cost of their freedom and for some their lives.[2]

Uprisings by colonized people are almost always as violent as they are inevitable. The colonizers want to hold onto power; the colonized want to administer and live in peace in their own country. At the very beginning of his influential book on colonization, *The Wretched of the Earth*, author Frantz Fanon writes: "National liberation, national renaissance, the restoration of nationhood to the people, commonwealth: whatever may be the headings used or the new formulas introduced, decolonization is always a violent phenomenon."[3] Uprisings succeed, as they did in India and in South Africa; they may, as in the case of the "Arab Spring," lead to less than desirable results. Violence, to one degree or another, on the part of one side or the other, or both, was always involved.

I want to focus on the Middle East, Algeria in particular. Algeria, a large Muslim and Berber country in North Africa, was invaded by the French in 1830. In a troubling parallel with South Africa, the colonialists settled within the country, though, unlike the Boers in South Africa, the French became the majority population and mingled with the very people they oppressed in a 130-year cycle of revolt and repression until they finally left in 1962. They left for some of the usual reasons—the country they occupied was no longer of use to them. But the main reason it was no longer of use was because the internal opposition grew too strong and persistent to suppress. The cycles of revolt and oppression took their toll on the occupiers. In France itself, the opposition to French rule in Algeria was all but overwhelming. Bombings and shootings by the Algerian Resistance had become a regular occurrence on the streets of Paris. On October 17, 1961, the police shot into a crowd of some 30,000 protesters and killed more than 200 people, throwing many of their bodies into the river Seine.[4]

There are two fascinating and powerful films about the Algerian war for independence. The most recent, *Caché* (*Hidden*), was made by the Austrian director Michael Haneke in 2005. A middle-class Parisian couple, Georges and Anne, keep receiving videotapes showing their house under surveillance. They have no idea who is taking and sending the images. As the narrative continues, we learn that Georges' parents had taken in an Algerian child whose own parents were killed by the police during the massacre of 1961. Georges visits that child, Majid, now a sad grown man, living in a tiny apartment. The result of Georges' probing and accusations causes a horrific moment—Majid slits his throat as Georges stands helplessly by, observing this act of defiance and self-hatred just as that mysterious camera watches Georges. But the tapes, the film suggests, are not to be taken literally. There is no mysterious person stalking Georges and his family. The tapes are images of Georges' and, by extension, France's bad conscience, a national outrage writ small as a family melodrama, a haunting by the past. Haneke is indicting bad faith and the erasure of memory; the inability to come to terms with a disastrous past which, like the return of the repressed, keeps impinging on those who try to forget.

The Battle of Algiers, a film directed by Gillo Pontecorvo in 1966, is a fictionalized documentation of the struggle of the FLN (the Algerian National Liberation Front) against the French force of occupation. The film emerges from of a period of intense political experimentation in European and, to a lesser extent, in American film, sparked somewhat by the worldwide political resistance to the Vietnam War. We will have an opportunity to address various aspects of this movement at different places and for various films further on. Here, it is important to understand the *form* of *The Battle of Algiers* as well as its content. I said that the film is a "fictionalized documentation," an interesting hybrid that has its origins in one of the most important movements in modern cinema: Italian neorealism. At the end of WWII, Italy and its filmmaking facilities lay in ruins. Cinecitta, a large studio founded by the fascist leader, Benito Mussolini, and his son Vittorio, was bombed out. To make movies, filmmakers—like Roberto Rossellini and Vittorio De Sica—took to the streets, used non-professional actors, and told stories about working people struggling in the war's aftermath. Many of their films, especially Rossellini's *Rome, Open City* (1945) and De Sica's *Bicycle Thieves* (1948) (Figure 5.1), have a raw immediacy, a feeling for the way environment, history, and character interact.

Figure 5.1 Life on the streets in the neorealist film *Bicycle Thieves*.

Rossellini's film was made as the Germans were fleeing Rome. He borrowed unused film stock from the U.S. Signal Corps. The film is unflinching in its view of German atrocities and at the same time tender toward the spirit of resistance and endurance of ordinary people. *Bicycle Thieves* focuses on one man whose livelihood—putting up posters of American movie stars—depends on his having a bike. When it is stolen, his small world collapses, and the film follows the peregrinations of him and his small son as they scour the poor sections of Rome trying to find the thief and the bike.

Neorealism was a political force on many levels. It was an attack on the glossy productions of Hollywood and pre-war Italian cinema. It focused on the working class, a group largely ignored by film no matter where it originates. In its ten-year life, neorealism produced something of a break in the history of film, and its influence was enormous. Even American film began shooting on location in an attempt to capture the grittiness of the neorealist mise-en-scène. *The Battle of Algiers* partakes of this influence and adds to it a documentary feel. Shot in grainy high-contrast black and white, loosely framed to convey the impression that it is recording events on the spot, using mostly non-professional actors and addressing a political reality, the film creates an illusion of a reality observed. It begins in the middle of things: an Algerian has just been tortured to reveal the hiding place of

Revolution in the 1960s 63

Figure 5.2 Ali le Pointe (Brahim Hadjadj) and his group of Resistance fighters hide behind a wall that is about to be blown up by the French military.

FLN member Ali le Pointe (Brahim Hadjadj), a second man, a woman, and a child, all members of the Resistance. The soldiers swarm the Casbah and surround the room, behind whose wall the four are hiding (Figure 5.2). The film then shifts to the beginning of the uprising, 1954, and the meeting of Ali, an illiterate, unemployed young man, with Jaffar, an organizer for the FLN.

Ali's induction into the revolutionary cause is a prelude to a series of events in which the fledgling group imposes Muslim restrictions on alcohol and drugs and undertakes a series of assassinations of colonial policemen. The events are told swiftly, each stamped with day, month, year, and time, and without passion or judgment. Policemen are shot: guns are hidden in trashcans; a woman in a white veil, a *haïk*, bitterly pushes off a policeman who tries to frisk her, and hands a gun to a co-conspirator, who shoots a cop. These acts are leavened by a brief sequence of an FLN-sanctioned marriage. All the while, information is relayed through voiceover announcements from the FLN or the police.

The participation of women in the Algerian Revolution was a stunning and somewhat traumatic event for both sides. Women in the Middle East are rarely permitted an active role in the affairs of men, so their participation in the Algerian uprising was both a surprise and a necessity. Frantz Fanon wrote about the participation of women in the uprising. His observations help clarify the situation of veiled women in Middle Eastern societies in general:

This woman who sees without being seen frustrates the colonizer. There is no reciprocity. She does not yield herself, does not give herself, does not offer herself. The Algerian has an attitude toward the Algerian woman—which is on the whole clear. He does not see her. There is even a permanent intention not to perceive the feminine profile, not to pay attention to the women.

But the Revolution demands a break not only with the colonial powers, but with cultural traditions as well. Fanon writes:

> The decision to involve women as active elements of the Algerian Revolution was not reached lightly. In a sense, it was the very conception of the combat that had to be modified. The violence of the occupier, his ferocity, his delirious attachment to the national territory, induced the leaders no longer to exclude certain forms of combat. Progressively, the urgency of a total war made itself felt. But involving the women was not solely a response to the desire to mobilize the entire nation. The women's entry into the war had to be harmonized with respect for the revolutionary nature of the war. In other words, the women had to show as much spirit of sacrifice as the men. It was therefore necessary to have the same confidence in them as was required from seasoned militants who had served several prison sentences. A moral elevation and a strength of character that were altogether exceptional would therefore be required of the women. There was no lack of hesitations. The revolutionary wheels had assumed such proportions; the mechanism was running at a given rate. The machine would have to be complicated; in other words its network would have to be extended without affecting its efficiency. The women could not be conceived of as a replacement product, but as an element capable of adequately meeting the new tasks.[5]

The "new tasks," the violence against the French, shake both sides out of their complacency. There are physical attacks, of course, but cultural and political attacks as well. The opposition takes advantage of weaknesses, of the colonial spaces themselves. The French residents and their police occupy open boulevards and apartment buildings. The French sit in outdoor cafés, emulating the life of European ease. They yell taunts at the native population. Some of the colonialists take violent action, bombing Algerian homes. The Algerians occupy the terraced warrens of the Casbah into which they disappear so the police cannot find them. When the Algerians get organized, the power shifts briefly to their hands. After a bombing attack by the French, Pontecorvo shows the devastation—dead children being carried out of the rubble—and makes a sharp cut to Ali leading a throng of Algerian men and women down the steps of the Casbah to avenge the murders. The little boy, Omar, who will figure in the Resistance, stops him, and Ali holds back the crowd until Jaffar himself appears, warning the angry mob that they will be slaughtered if they proceed.

What the enraged native population learns is that, at the start of their rebellion against their colonial masters, they are in a weak position. The colonizers own the means of mass retaliation; military power is on their side. The response, therefore, has to be limited, individual, unexpected violent action: terror attacks in the form of bombings of public places—carried out by women. The women shed their hajibs, cut and dye their hair, put on makeup. They turn, externally, into Westerners. Some Frenchmen flirt with them, and all this allows them to get through the blockade of soldiers at the exit way from the Casbah. A bomb is planted in a bar, in a teenage dance hall, in the airport ticket office of Air France. We witness the first two bombs explode and only hear the third. Pontecorvo lingers briefly on the carnage the bombings leave behind, at one point playing the mournful melody heard over the bombing in the Casbah earlier. (The score for the film was written by Pontecorvo and by Ennio Morricone. Their percussive drumbeats accompany most of the preparations for the bombings.)

The bombings occur midway through *The Battle of Algiers* and mark a pivot in the struggle. French paratroopers, led by Col. Philippe Mathieu (Jean Matthew)—himself a former Resistance fighter during WWII and a veteran of the French defeat in Vietnam in the battle of Dien Bien Fu—march through the city, preparing to quell the uprising. (We have already caught a brief glimpse of Mathieu at the beginning of the film, whose narrative is circular, ending where it began.) Mathieu wears dark glasses indoors and out, giving him an air of supercilious mystery but also, perhaps, indicating his blindness to the power of the uprising he is attempting to quell. This blindness is proven in a sequence in which Pontecorvo presents a film within the film. Mathieu shows his men footage he's had taken of Arabs descending from the Casbah through the military's checkpoints. And while he's commenting on how difficult it is to recognize the individuals committing violence, one of the women carrying the bomb looks and smiles at the camera.

This film within a film is a fascinating gesture. On the surface, it is a kind of spit in the eye of the colonial authorities who have come to quell the revolt. But it also points to the artifice of the film itself.

The Battle of Algiers uses documentary techniques to make it appear as if it were shot within the swirl of actual events, and then presents another fake documentary within the "fake" documentary that is *The Battle of Algiers* itself. The brief smile on the face of the woman bomber in the military's film not only mocks them, but is a kind of wink to the viewer herself. This reflexivity—film reflecting itself *as film* to the viewer—is a common technique in the experimental cinema of the 1960s, and we will see it again as filmmakers themselves reflect on the politics of viewing.

The woman's glance is also a sign of confidence in what will become an increasingly desperate struggle as Mathieu ratchets up his repression—through torture. The FLN has right and justice on their side. The organization's head, Ben M'hidi, explains: "It's hard enough to start a revolution, even harder enough to sustain it, and the hardest of all to win it." To prove his point, and in the face of the United Nations that has called a meeting to discuss the Algerian question, and Mathieu's promise to round up Arabs and torture them into giving up their leaders, the FLN call a general strike. The military responds with the only thing they have: brute force. They round up the strikers and smash their shops. We see another result of torture, the sufferer made to broadcast a call to give up the strike and denounce the FLN. This is leavened when Omar, the small boy fighting for the cause, steals the microphone to give courage to the strikers.

Bombings continue. Ben M'hidi is captured and we are told that he hanged himself in his cell. Mathieu, at a press conference, defends torture, and at this point makes visible what Pontecorvo has withheld for the length of the film: showing torture itself, which, even simulated for a movie, is a risky move. It can arouse those of a sadistic bent (certain modern horror films have been called "torture porn"), but will more likely appall a viewer and make him turn away. There are very few scenes of torture in the history of film that are successful in causing not only disgust but a certain understanding of the absolute depravity of the people who commit it. Such is the case in Roberto Rossellini's *Rome, Open City*, the neorealist film mentioned earlier. Here a Resistance fighter is brutally tortured by the Nazis and the effect on the viewer is astonished pity for the victim and overwhelming anger at the perpetrators. Similarly, in *The Battle of Algiers*, the mercifully brief images of torture are difficult to watch. They are accompanied by mournful music on the soundtrack, which has the effect of guiding our emotions away from repulsion and toward sadness and pity. Shots of the tearful face of an Algerian woman further channel the impact because her grief becomes a surrogate for our own.

In their growing anger and desperation, the Resistance takes to gunning down Europeans on the streets and bombing soldiers. At one point, Pontecorvo freezes the frame when a truck driven by Algerians purposefully plows into a crowd of Frenchmen, as if asking us to ponder this brutal and desperate act.[6] The military continues their attacks, finally cornering Ali, Omar, Mahmud, and the woman, Hassiba (Jaffar has already been taken into captivity), who have hidden behind a wall in a room in the Casbah. We have come full circle. The pitiable little man, tortured into revealing their hiding place, is forced by the soldiers to point it out. It is a final act of humiliation. The military blow up the hiding place while Mathieu and his general watch from a safe distance. A cameraman films the event. Algerians watch and pray. A baby cries. The military men congratulate themselves.

A film about revolution cannot end with the failure of the revolution. The circular narrative of *The Battle of Algiers* inscribes a point from which there is a return. After the FLN hierarchy is destroyed, the people again take to the streets. The film ends a few years after the main narrative of events with a spontaneous demonstration by the Algerians. With flags made of sheets and rags, the men chanting for freedom, the women ululating, they crowd the streets and defy the soldiers shooting them down, finally emerging from the smoke of colonial rule, proclaiming their freedom, a woman dancing and waving a homemade flag (Figure 5.3). A title tells us that Algeria achieved freedom from the French in 1962.

Figure 5.3 The people of Algiers emerge *en masse* to reclaim their country.

The country has had a somewhat rocky history since its independence—a coup, a military takeover, an assassinated leader, economic difficulties, demands for recognition by its Berber population, attacks by Al Qaeda—but in the end, it has maintained a largely democratic government, stained to some extent by a history of human trafficking. Despite all that, it is a country of some stability in an unstable region.[7]

The film, *The Battle of Algiers*, has had a curious afterlife. It was, perhaps unsurprisingly, banned by France for a few years. Perhaps very surprisingly, it has been screened at the Pentagon to demonstrate terrorism and counterterrorism techniques.[8] It is an ironic testament to the film's force that this fictionalized narrative could be used to teach the realities of global struggle. It is ironic as well that the view of revolutionary struggle taken by the film has become inverted by being used to teach how to squelch revolutionary struggle. And while Algeria itself is a fairly settled country politically, throughout the region, terrorism committed by extremists threatens not only their own countries, but countries worldwide. The acts of violence committed by the Algerians against their oppressors have morphed into brutal acts of violence by rulers against their own people, as in the case of Syria, and attacks on domestic and foreign populations in the name of the Islamic State. Does the film teach us about the methods of terrorism and counterterrorism—as the Pentagon might have thought—or does it demonstrate where violent acts of rebellion might be justified? Can violence ever be justified? How else can the unbearable anger and frustration of a colonized people be expressed against the colonizers who hold all the power?

The Battle of Algiers answers these questions unambiguously. Pontecorvo does not shrink from showing the devastation visited on the French by the shootings and bombings carried out by the FLN; however, these victims are not personalized, unlike the Algerians, whose faces and names we know and who, throughout the course of the film, become sympathetic characters. Col. Mathieu is not. To put it in terms familiar to this book, *The Battle of Algiers* is an unapologetic political film, and its politics are left of center. Its form as an engaging, suspenseful, quasi-documentary exposition and representation of events in a revolution marks it as a film not only about politics, but political in its very form. The French filmmaker, Jean-Luc Godard (whose films we will examine in Chapter 7), once said that it is important not merely to make political films, but to make films politically. This is a notion we have been thinking about and will continue to investigate.

Notes

1 For a brief history of the British in India see www.bbc.co.uk/history/british/modern/independence1947_01.shtml.
2 A chronology of events in South Africa is at www.bbc.com/news/world-africa-14094918.
3 Frantz Fanon, *The Wretched of the Earth*, trans. Constance Farrington (New York: Grove Press, 1963), 35.
4 A detailed history of Algeria is at www.historyworld.net/wrldhis/PlainText Histories.asp?ParagraphID=okz.
5 Frantz Fanon, *A Dying Colonialism*, trans. Haakon Chevalier (New York: Grove Press, 1965), 44, 48.
6 See Joan Mellon, *Filmguide to* The Battle of Algiers (Bloomington, IN: Indiana University Press, 1973), 36. Also Tony Shaw, *Cinematic Terror: A Global History of Terrorism on Film* (New York: Bloomsbury, 2014), 82–101.
7 See the link in note 4.
8 See www.nytimes.com/2003/09/07/weekinreview/the-world-film-studies-what-does-the-pentagon-see-in-battle-of-algiers.html.

Further reading

A discussion of the film and the history it attempts to narrate is at www.opendemocracy.net/martin-evans/battle-of-algiers-historical-truth-and-filmic-representation.
Gary Crowdus, "Terrorism and Torture in *The Battle of Algiers*: An Interview with Saadi Yacef," *Cinéaste*, vol. 29, no. 3, Summer 2004, pp. 30–37.
Frantz Fanon, *The Wretched of the Earth*, trans. Constance Farrington (New York: Grove Press, 1963), 35.
—— *A Dying Colonialism*, trans. Haakon Chevalier (New York: Grove Press, 1965), 44, 48.
Joan Mellon, *Filmguide to* The Battle of Algiers (Bloomington, IN: Indiana University Press, 1973).
David Overby, trans. and ed., *Springtime in Italy: A Reader on Neo-Realism* (Hamden, CT: Archon Books, 1979).
Tony Shaw, *Cinematic Terror: A Global History of Terrorism on Film* (New York: Bloomsbury, 2014).

6 Revolutionary cinema in Latin America
Lucía (1968)

The Battle of Algiers is a film about a pre-revolutionary moment, or perhaps a *pro*-revolutionary moment. It is also very much a film of its time. The 1960s were, as we will continue to see, a period of political upheaval over large parts of the world. At the core of this upheaval, in the West, was the Vietnam War. Elsewhere, in Latin America, for example, there were countries suffering under repressive regimes, as in Brazil, or, like Chile, where, in 1973, a democratically elected leftist government was violently overturned by a U.S.-backed coup. It put in place a vicious dictator. Right-wing oppression seemed to dominate many Latin American countries with death squads assassinating leftists or the military throwing victims out of planes, where "the disappeared" referred to people spirited off by the government, never to be seen again.

Despite all this, filmmaking flourished in some Latin American countries (or, in the case of Chile, by filmmakers who escaped the clutches of Augusto Pinochet's government and worked in exile). Brazilian filmmakers, before and during the rule of the generals, founded a movement called *Cinema Novo*. Drawing on the principles of Italian neorealism, these filmmakers concentrated on the poor and dispossessed, especially in Brazil's impoverished northeast; some drew on folk myths and incorporated music and dance within a melodramatic framework. No one exemplified this better than Glauber Rocha, whose great film *António das Mortes* (1969) goes beyond neorealism to become an extraordinary mixture of history lesson, folklore, song, operatic melodrama, gunplay, knife play, and revolutionary passion imaged through the story of St. George and the Dragon set in the wastelands of northeast Brazil. It is an outrageous, almost surreal work, hard to find these days (there is a fuzzy copy on YouTube), but so fully representative of the best revolutionary cinema that it is worth searching out.

Of all Latin American countries making movies during the 1960s, none was more active, varied, and inventive than Cuba. This small island, 90 miles off the coast of Florida, sharing some of its land with the infamous U.S. detention center at the Guantánamo Bay Naval Base, has remained a Communist stronghold since the Revolution of 1959. Throughout the Cold War, when anti-Communism was the dominant discourse of U.S. foreign and, to a great extent, domestic policy, when anti-Communism was (as we will see in Chapters 9 and 10) the common coin of American life in general, Cuba remained a Communist thorn. While the U.S. trained right-wing death squads in other Latin American countries, Cuba, under USSR patronage and support, supplied medical care for its citizens and all but wiped out illiteracy. It also attempted to export revolution to other countries, which did not add to its popularity. Yes, the revolutionary Cuban government suppressed dissent and jailed many of those who spoke out against the regime. It held a defensive posture against the United States, which tried to destroy it after the Revolution, and which kept a trade embargo against the country until the present moment. Only recently and briefly has something of a détente been created between the two countries.

Cuba has endured, but as its economy faltered after the fall of the Soviet Union, its filmmaking faded. Before the fade out, however, came some of the richest experiments in the lively cinema of the 1960s and 70s. Within months of the Revolution, the new government set up ICAIC (Instituto Cubano de Arte e Industria Cinematográficos) to oversee film production. This was not to be the production of conventional cinema. Like the Italian filmmakers after WWII (whose neorealist style was a big influence on Cuban filmmakers, as it was the world over), they would start anew, start by dissecting cinematic conventions themselves. Alfredo Guevara (no relation to the revolutionary Che Guevara), head of ICAIC, said that their purpose was "to demystify cinema for the entire population; to work, in a way, against our own power; to reveal all the tricks, all the resources of language; to dismantle all the mechanisms of cinematic hypnosis."[1] The comment recalls the work of the German playwright, Bertolt Brecht, who we mentioned briefly in Chapter 2. Brecht insisted that a work of art should not fool the viewer into being a passive observer of an illusion of reality but rather educate her in the mechanisms and the politics of illusion.

The Other Francisco (Sergio Giral, 1974) begins as an overblown melodrama about a slave and his lover. The slave, Francisco, hangs himself when he discovers his lover has slept with her master.

Everything—music, gestures, camera movements—is overwrought. Something is wrong. The narrative makes a sudden shift to a 19th-century drawing room where an actor portraying Anselmo Suárez y Romero, the author of Cuba's first anti-slavery novel, is reading to his guests. The narrator tells us that the guests and the author are in a state of self-congratulation because liberal businessmen brought slavery in Cuba to an end when they came to realize that slavery was bad for business. They discovered that it was cheaper to pay poor wages to people of African descent than to support them as enslaved people. The narrator asks if there is another Francisco, closer to the reality of slavery in Cuba and the economic self-interest that allowed the keeping of slaves and then found it more economical to free them. Would the real Francisco have hanged himself for love? The rest of the film goes on to represent the horrible brutalities of slavery. Slaves did commit suicide as an act of rebellion. But they also revolted against their masters. We are witness to revolution and counter-revolution in all its cruelties.[2]

The film is didactic in the best sense of the word: it engages and tells us historical truths. It entertains and then asks us to interrogate our entertainment to find that it is based on a misreading of history. It recognizes that melodrama is always a diversion whose exaggerations need to be understood as lies—entertaining lies, but lies all the same. In short, we cannot always believe what we see in a movie, and if we exercise active viewing, *political* viewing, the entertainment will not fade but only become more informed.

The Other Francisco is just one of many films produced by ICAIC during the golden age of Cuban cinema. Not all were as openly didactic, but most—both fiction films and documentaries—attempted to present the revolutionary society not only in its best light, but in a light that clarified the issues confronting what was essentially a new society. Among those films one stands out as the great epic of this period: Humberto Solás's 1968 film, *Lucía*. Just short of three hours in length, *Lucía* consists of three parts. The first takes place in 1895, when Cuba was struggling against Spanish rule. The second is set in 1932, when there was a strong movement to overthrow the dictator Gerardo Machado, whose rule was ultimately brought to an end by American interference, only to usher in Fulgencio Batista, whose oppressive reign was brought to an end by Fidel Castro's Revolution. The third part of the film takes place in the post-revolutionary moment when women were struggling against the ingrained culture of machismo. One woman is prominent in each of the sections, each named Lucía. She is the unthinking victim of Spanish oppression in the first part, the frightened partner of a fighter against Machado in the second, and finally, a rural worker—a campesina—struggling with her husband for equality.

Each section places Lucía in a different class: aristocrat, member of the lower middle class, rural worker. Each section is done in a different style and genre: the first a parody of a costume melodrama with touches of violent battle and even magical realism; the second something approaching a political thriller; and the third a free-wheeling battle of the sexes. In each, Solás and his collaborators and actors create not only sets and costumes reminiscent of the period, but camera strategies, gestures, and facial expressions that indicate the period and its discontents. The film's politics lie not only in its subject matter, but in its mise-en-scène—the spatial construction of the images. There is no question of "realism" here. Solás allows the viewer access to the artificiality of the film by means of its exaggerations, its melodrama, its acknowledgment that, past, present, or future, a film represents the times it tells only in images that aren't an approximation but a provocation.

For example, the flutterings of the women in their sewing room early in the first section of the film, taking place in 1895, filmed in low-contrast black and white, are interrupted by a straight cut to an overhead shot of an oxcart carrying a near naked corpse. The following images of Spanish soldiers are shown in harsh, high-contrast images as they straggle home from battle. The music is grim and discordant. We are introduced to a dirt-encrusted woman dressed in black, lying on the ground. This is Fernandina, Lucía's double, the chthonic feminine force of Cuba. As the upper-class ladies flutter about and run to the window to look, Fernandina runs crazily through the streets, yelling at Cubans to wake up.

One of the aristocratic women tells the tale of Fernandina, that she was a nun ministering to dead soldiers, and Solás cuts to an even harsher image of wailing nuns in glaring white habits on the smoking wastelands of the battlefield. Bodies hang from a scaffold. Suddenly one of the bodies springs to life; bandits appear and violently strip and rape the nuns. The soundtrack echoes their screams; the upper-class ladies are in tears over the story. The violence Solás addresses here is not only the violence he is showing on the screen, but the violent separation of the upper class from the struggles happening on the ground, violence they have walled off from their lives. The ladies are dressed in white while the white habits of the nuns are torn from them in the dirt.

Inevitably, there has to be a joining of these worlds. White and black, Cuban aristocracy and Cuban peasant and fighter, heaven and earth. And this must occur through Lucía (here played by Raquel Revuelta), who meets her treacherous lover-to-be, Rafael, at church, setting up a massive balloon of melodrama that will inevitably need to be punctured. The warning signs come early. Rafael, part Spanish, part Cuban, claims political neutrality. Within left-wing ideology, stating that one is apolitical sets off immediate alarms. No one is apolitical; no one can be effectually neutered and removed from the world where politics on the macro and micro level influence everyone and every action. It is not possible to be apolitical, and stating so is not a neutral gesture but usually a lie.

Suspicions are raised immediately, as Rafael tries to get information about Lucía's plantation in the hills, and about her brother, Felipe, bearded, looking like a contemporary Cuban revolutionary before the fact. But Lucía is blinded by love—literally so as she dances blindfolded with her girlfriends. There is something structurally odd about this particular sequence. Lucía is blindfolded, but Solás, following the women around the room, intercuts shots of Lucía from her point of view even though, given that she is blindfolded, it's an impossible point of view. She could not see her friends whirling around her. The point is that if only Lucía could see, she might recognize the threat posed by Rafael. But the fog of melodramatic romance prevents this. Melodrama is a genre that imposes excess and blindness upon its characters and its audience. Melodrama begs us not to see past its excess; the strain to bursting of its outsized emotions hides its misdirection, its utter impossibility, its political mischief.[3]

We learn from two gossips in the street—in a sequence that has the mad Fernandina assaulted by drunkards—that Rafael has a wife and child in Spain. We don't learn how Lucía finds this out, but can assume that in her circle, gossip is rife. Lucía is too besotted with Rafael and allows the melodrama to swallow her whole, and she meets her lover in a series of abandoned ruins, where Solás uses the same high-contrast, hand-held style that he has used for the Fernandina sequences, with the addition of swelling music and much passionate abandon. At one point, Lucía drags her arm across her forehead in a gesture as old as melodrama itself. She rips open Rafael's shirt to a burst of music and Solás cuts to a shot of a tower rising high above the trees, as the two lovers are seen as tiny figures below. This is extreme parody of melodrama's excess, of the telenovelas so popular in Latin American, of patriarchal power, and a warning of the disaster to come. Lucía will take Rafael to the secret coffee plantation, despite being accosted in the street by the mad Fernandina, who, as Lucía's more prescient double, knows what's to come.

Rafael is, of course, a Spanish spy. He and Lucía's journey to the mountains is pursued by Spanish troops, who take part in a gruesome battle with Cuban forces, bodies slogging through the mud and blood. Solás does not allow this ambush to go unanswered, and the remarkable battle is followed by something more remarkable still: on horseback, naked African-Cuban warriors enter the battle fighting hand to hand on the land and in the water. It is an extraordinary scene that extends the metaphor of the earth as the origin of Cuba's strength. Through it all, Lucía wanders amidst the battle and its dead, her brother Felipe's corpse among them. In her distraction, she is slowly turning into Fernandina, a conjunction, consummated at the end of the film, necessary to indicate the revolutionary dissolution of the ruling class. The visual quality of the image becomes more drained of gray-tones, more starkly black and white. The music is more and more discordant. The climax is reached as an old woman tells Lucía where to find Rafael, who is in the town square amidst a wildly abandoned celebration. She does find him and stabs him over and over, both of them collapsing; Lucía's head, her eyes glassy and afraid, is cradled in Fernandina's hands (Figure 6.1). Solás freezes the frame.

The first section of Lucía observes and represents the past as a period of delirium. It is not merely made up of betrayals, bad faith, and desperate mistakes, but of heroic resistance emerging from the very soil of a beleaguered country in dizzying battles for its independence. The second section, labeled "1932," is calmer, steadier in approach.

Figure 6.1 The three Lucías: cradled in Fernandina's hands after stabbing Rafael at the end of the 1895 episode (Raquel Revuelta).

76 *Revolutionary cinema in Latin America*

Solás tends to use a zoom lens rather than the frenzied movements of the hand-held camera employed in the first section. Except for certain scenes, the narrative is itself less frenzied, more contemplative, its events told in a series of flashbacks recalled by this Lucía (Eslinda Núñez). Her 1932 incarnation works in a tobacco factory, and the film pieces together her life from her idle middle-class days arguing with a gossipy, fussy mother to her love for Aldo, who is part of the struggle against the Machado dictatorship, which is shown with subdued violence. Scenes of everyday life and affection play out over the fight for freedom. Lucía and her friend scrawl anti-Machado graffiti on the bathroom wall of the cigar factory. Aldo and his friends raid a gathering of police in an amusement hall.

The raid is intercut with a march by Lucía and her friends that is brutally attacked by the police. Some of the police are shot by Aldo and his two colleagues, but a large gathering of protestors are attacked and beaten on the street. This sequence of events is told in the most energetic style of the 1932 section. Rapid editing communicates the frenzy of the attacks. Machado is overthrown and forced to leave the country when the military itself revolts against his rule. The little group of Aldo, Lucía, and their friends celebrate. But the liberation is not liberating. Aldo pushes paper in his bureaucratic office, hoping to move up in the government. His friend, Antonio, is having an affair. Lucía is pregnant. This brief interlude is but a prelude to the rule of Fulgencio Batista. Aldo is depressed by the decadence of Havana. Sickened by rum and despair, he tries to revive the revolutionary spirit, but his energy is gone and his despair poisons his relationship with Lucía. He tries one more raid and is killed. We see only the results: Aldo on a slab in the morgue and Lucía in hysterics. We last see her walking by a stand of derelict buildings by the water, lost and alone. She stares directly at us and Solás fades to black (Figure 6.2).

The differences in closure of the first two sections of *Lucía* are important. The violent ending of the first part ends with a freeze frame of Lucía's face cradled in the hands of Fernandina. It is an oddly optimistic ending, portending as it does the absorption of the aristocratic class back into the bedrock of Cuban life and, of course, the destruction of Spanish rule. The fade to black that closes on Lucía's sad gaze at the camera at the end of the second section seems much more pessimistic, considering that the Castro Revolution would be thirty years in the future. Perhaps Solás is reminding his home audience that the Batista years that followed Machado were especially grim, with Cuba reduced to something approaching a debauched colony of the United States. The Batista reign was indeed a fade to black, and Solás

Revolutionary cinema in Latin America 77

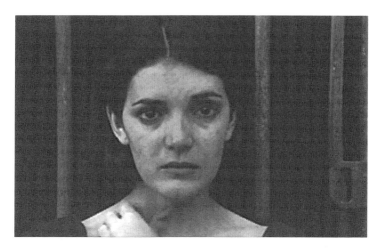

Figure 6.2 Distraught after the loss of Aldo at the end of the 1932 episode (Eslinda Núñez).

is depending on his audience knowing what happened to bring the darkness to light.

The last section of the film, entitled "196__," occurs after the Revolution. It has happened, and the job of Cubans is to move forward and liberate themselves. The two incarnations of Lucía we have seen so far were undone by men and events out of their control. The ideal of the Revolution is to give that control back to the people and, in this film especially, to women. National liberation can occur, the film asserts, only when individual liberation and especially the liberation of the sexes occurs.

For the most part, the style of the last section is brighter in its use of black and white, easier and freer in its camera movements, and, excluding its crisis, easier in the movement and comportment of its characters. The Lucía of this section (Adela Legrá) is not of the aristocracy, not of the middle class, not an urban worker. She is a rural, creole campesina, a peasant working the fields and, in good revolutionary style, happy with her work and her sister workers. The music for much of the sequence is a version of the popular Cuban song, Guantanamera, here with lyrics that narrate the film: the joy of the countryside and working the earth. (With the exception of Guantanamera, the extraordinary music for the film was composed by Leo Brouwer.) The whole atmosphere of this sequence is bright and full of optimism, despite the questionable, often violent tactics of Lucía's husband, Tomás.

Lucía is newly married to this cigar-smoking worker who wants to exercise his machismo to an extraordinary degree. He is jealous. He gets into fights when another man dances with his wife at a party. He doesn't want Lucía to work; he doesn't want her to leave the house. When she tells her friend Angelina that she can't go back into the fields, Angelina asks "What about the Revolution?" But Solás is asking not only about the Revolution, but about how gender equality can work under any circumstances. He is addressing Cuba in the flush of post-revolutionary excitement, when it was necessary for everyone who was able to go to work for the good of the country. But he is also addressing the wider issue of male privilege and its overweening, indeed stifling burden.

Literally stifling in the case of Lucía and Tomás. He locks her in the house and nails the windows shut. When the literacy teacher arrives from Havana to teach Lucía to read and write (part of the country-wide literacy program initiated by Castro), Tomás denies him access. His friend Flavio tries to explain that the literacy campaign is a revolutionary act, that it frees people from "Yankee imperialism." More immediately, it is an act of personal freedom as well as a break from the past. Tomás's father treated his mother badly, and by extension the pre-revolutionary treatment of women in general saw them treated badly. Tomás proves a very difficult case. He beats up the literacy teacher in a scene filled with hysterical screaming that results in Lucía escaping the house. And when Lucía finally learns to write, she can release herself from Tomás's jealous tyranny. She leaves Tomás a note: "I'm going. I'm not a slave." He chases her to the salt flats, where she has gone to work. The women workers wrestle Tomás to the ground while Lucía screams that she does not love him anymore. He degenerates into the town drunk.

But there is something wrong with all of this: the music. It is light and frothy. When Guantanemara returns again, the singer tells us about Tomás's fall and his mistakes. Throughout this sequence, there may be much yelling and some abuse, but there is not the melodrama that marked its first two parts. Old ways are changing; the Revolution has changed them. We last see Lucía and Tomás arguing by the sea, and there is a specter, a young girl wrapped in a white head scarf, leading a goat and seen, by means of a telephoto lens, as if she were simultaneously near and far. She is the Lucía to come. She looks at the Lucía of the present and Tomás, still struggling, yelling, the camera circling them; but she sees them from the future. We see her in closeup and then a point-of-view to Lucía and Tomás fighting by the ocean (Figure 6.3). The music rises to a rousing crescendo; the Lucía of the future laughs and runs off. The screen fades to white.

Figure 6.3 Struggling for her rights at the end of the contemporary episode (Adela Legrá).

Right-wing cinema may end with defeat of the enemy—often a minority group—and an emphasis on the dark power of the nation being celebrated. Populist cinema pulls out a victory for the downtrodden at the last minute. Conventional Hollywood cinema celebrates successful heterosexual romance or a hero who struggles successfully against an all but insuperable enemy. Left-wing revolutionary cinema looks to the past as prelude and the revolutionary present as a consummation of past struggles while insisting on continued progress. *Triumph of the Will* is a steady drumbeat of straight-jacketed authoritarianism; *Battleship Potemkin* celebrates communal revolt against the regime; *Mr. Smith Goes to Washington* cries out for the simple wisdom and triumph of the "common man." The 2016 *The Birth of a Nation* demands the necessity of rebellion despite the overwhelming odds of its failure. *Lucía* celebrates revolution by examining Cuba's tortured past and emphasizing a better future. It avoids the grand statements of Eisenstein's film by concentrating on the matter of gender. Rather than Eisensteinian montage, and more like *Battle of Algiers*, Humberto Solás uses a variety of camera strategies to imagine historical events and create moods of melodrama, hysteria, darkness, and, finally, the light of the future. Like Pontecorvo, he deals with gender and with race (the last section of the film is populated by black and creole people working together). And, however high the pitch of hysteria becomes between the characters within the film, the film itself takes an assured view, stimulating the viewer, inciting thought, playing with cinematic convention. Being progressive.

The future of Cuban cinema and ICAIC was not a straight line of success. Struggles over funding and internal politics, reorganizations, controversies over what kinds of films were to be made, and a dropoff in audience all led to a loss in the power of experimentation that occurred in the 1960s and early 70s.[4] Yet Humberto Solás continued his work, making a huge historical film about Chile and the massacre of miners during a 1907 strike, *Cantata de Chile*, in 1976. As late as 1990, Cuban directors Tomás Gutiérrez Alea and Juan Carlos Tabío, in a co-production with Mexico and Spain, made an Academy Award nominee, *Strawberry and Chocolate*. Still, the great period of Cuban filmmaking was over, a fact that cannot be seen in isolation. Experimental, revolutionary filmmaking went into eclipse the world over by the 1980s, though political filmmaking continued and has reached something of a peak in recent years. We will continue analyzing the experimental period in the following chapter.

Notes

1 Quoted in John Mraz, "Lucia: Visual Style and Historical Portrayal," *Jump Cut*, 19, December 1978, 21.
2 For a full discussion of this and other Cuban films see Robert Phillip Kolker, *The Altering Eye: Contemporary International Cinema* (Cambridge, UK: Open Book Publishers, 2009), https://doi.org/10.11647/OBP.0002.
3 So much has been written on melodrama. A good place to start is the collection *Imitations of Life: A Reader on Film and Television Melodrama*, ed. Marcia Landy (Detroit, MI: Wayne State University Press (January 1, 1991).
4 The history of ICAIC can be found in Michael Chanon, *The Cuban Image* (London and Bloomington, IN: BFI Publishing and University of Indiana Press, 1985).

Further reading

Julianne Burton, ed., *Cinema and Social Change in Latin America: Conversations with Filmmakers* (Austin, TX: University of Texas Press, 1986).
Michael Chanon, *The Cuban Image* (London and Bloomington, IN: BFI Publishing and University of Indiana Press, 1985).
—— *Cultural Studies of the Americas: Cuban Cinema* (Minneapolis, MN: University of Minnesota Press, 2004).
John Mraz, "*Lucia*: Visual Style and Historical Portrayal," *Jump Cut*, 19, December 1978. www.ejumpcut.org/archive/jc50.2008/Lucia.

7 Politics and the apocalypse
Weekend (1967)

As noted in the previous chapters, the spirit of cinematic experimentation spread widely across the globe in the 1960s. France spearheaded the movement, and to understand that we need to pick up the narrative of postwar film history. Italian neorealism was very much a political movement, taking a stand against the form and content of Hollywood and Hollywood-influenced films that came before it, and facing the political wrath of the Italian government that did not like the way these films portrayed Italy. Neorealism ran its course in about ten years and there was a lull in unconventional filmmaking during much of the 1950s—but not a lull in the politics surrounding film, particularly in France.

After WWII, France became inundated with American films of the 1940s which had been embargoed during the Nazi occupation. Several things occurred in response: the French government set up a quota system that guaranteed that French films would be seen on French screens along with the more popular American movies. In response, many French filmmakers made high-toned adaptations of literary classics, fascinating if somewhat stodgy films that were dubbed "The Tradition of Quality." At the same time, a group of young filmmakers gathered at the Paris Cinémateque where films were shown all day long. They watched the newly available American movies and, despite their lack of English, discovered a vitality in these films absent from those made in their own country. They also noticed that, no matter who wrote or starred in a film, no matter the studio that produced it, films seemed to cohere in style and theme around the name of its director. From this observation came the auteur theory, *la politique des auteurs*, that changed filmmaking and the way it was studied. American film now had the advantage of a proper name: Alfred Hitchcock, Orson Welles, Howard Hawks, Nicholas Ray, among others, known and unknown in their native country.

82 Politics and the apocalypse

These young men evolved from rabid filmgoers to film critics, and they gravitated to André Bazin, the great film critic of the late 1940s and early 1950s. They wrote for his publications, developing the auteur theory, praising American film, condemning the French Tradition of Quality, and preparing for their own break into filmmaking. When they did, when François Truffaut, Claude Chabrol, Jacques Rivette, Eric Rohmer, and Jean-Luc Godard made their first films in the late 1950s and early 1960s, they became known collectively as the New Wave, and they changed cinema for a second time after WWII. Their love for American movies led some of them to make gangster films, others to absorb the style of Alfred Hitchcock; one, Jacques Rivette, made a film in 1979, *Out 1*, that ran for twelve hours. Of all the group, the most influential, the most daring and political, was Jean-Luc Godard, who is still making films almost sixty years later.

It is Godard who made the statement that it was not sufficient to make political films, but to make films politically.[1] To do that required a revolution in form that went far back into film history as well as to the theories of Bertolt Brecht, who spoke about breaking the illusion of reality to understand the workings of the work of art. It also required a confluence of political events: the French government's attempt to close the Paris Cinématèque and fire its director, Henri Langlois, in 1968, an act that brought people out on the streets to protest; the Vietnam War, which had already sparked demonstrations; and a general dissatisfaction with the state of French political culture. All of this led to the student uprising that, in 1968, nearly brought down the French government and that reverberated across the world and into the arts. Filmmakers especially began to rethink their cultural and political role and methods, and no one more thoroughly than Godard.

Godard liked to say that, in making his films, he had to start from zero, to think about film as if it had not been invented yet.[2] He wanted, even before the 1968 uprising, nothing less than a revolutionary rethinking of what film had to say and how it said it. To understand this, we have to once again go back to the beginning to get an idea of what Godard was thinking.

Film was one of the great technological inventions of the 19th century. Along with the telephone and radio, it was a product of modernity, of a world in which space and time were being altered by the technologies that seemed to shrink them, when cities, in all their chaos, became the hubs of civilization. It was a time of radical change and upheaval—a condition being repeated, under very different circumstances and for different reasons, during the 1968 uprisings. One response to modernity is the imaginative art of the modern, called modernism. To understand modernism, think about abstract expressionist painting that focuses on the formal elements of the medium: color, line, and volume instead of portraits or landscapes. Meaning lies in the artist's means of expression. Form over content. But what happens in film, which, from its beginnings at the end of the 19th century, wants to use its formal properties to represent the "real" world and tell stories? Film, it seems, is modernity without modernism, though with important exceptions. We have seen how Sergei Eisenstein fractured the continuity style of Hollywood filmmaking—the style that represents cinematic "reality." He breaks apart time and space while telling the story of a shipboard uprising in *Battleship Potemkin*—an event in a revolution that itself fractured the time of the old regime and its political space. Eisenstein made political films politically. Orson Welles's *Citizen Kane* (1941) is a film that is political in the sense that it looks at the life of a powerful public individual, but political as well in the ways it goes against the conventional style of filmmaking at the time. Welles uses techniques that emphasize the depth of cinematic space. He experiments with narrative time so that the film is told from multiple points of view, from the various people who knew Charles Foster Kane and have their own view of him. It is like a narrative jigsaw puzzle. *Citizen Kane* is not an avant-garde film, but it challenges assumptions of what Hollywood cinema can do and how much an audience will be willing to work with the new formal structures of the film.

It could be argued that film noir, the darkly shadowed, violent genre that took over American cinema from the mid-1940s to the early 1950s, was a modernist form. Diverging sharply from the optimism and redemption offered by so much of American film, noir spoke to the darkness and anxiety of the post-WWII state of mind. Male characters were portrayed as weak and brutalized; women as powerful and deadly. Noir turned the givens of American film upside down, from bright to dark, and had an influence on the French New Wave.

Godard's modernism was of a different order. Closer to the literature of James Joyce and T. S. Eliot, and to the hyper-real canvases of Andy Warhol (the maker of images of Campbell soup cans), the films of Godard's first period, from 1959 to the late 1960s, examined all the givens of traditional cinema. His films are heavily allusive. Allusion is an important element of modernist art. Because it foregrounds the formal properties of its discipline, modernism recognizes other works that are part of that discipline in a kind of creative continuity. For example, T. S. Eliot's poetry pulls in lines from other poets in an attempt to link the universe of poetry and recognize that an individual poet and his or her work is part of a community of poets and their work. Godard feels the same about moviemaking. His films are full of verbal and visual allusions to other films and to the act of filmmaking itself. In addition to its allusive structure, Godard films are fond of interrupting their narrative flow with a cartoon or advertising image, or a title that either reflects what is going on in the film or points in other directions. The intent is to call attention to the formal attributes of film: to make the audience pay attention not merely to what the film is talking about, but how it is talking about it. In fact, in doing all this, he is not quite going back to zero, but to the work and theories of Brecht.

Bertolt Brecht called for theatrical techniques that redirected viewers' attention away from being absorbed in the work, forgetting that it was a work. He wanted his audience to be aware that a work of art was *artificial* and therefore they must be aware of its artificiality and, ultimately, its politics. He used various methods such as deliberately artificial acting, flashing movies behind the action, and having actors break their role and address the audience. Similarly, Godard wanted the viewer to acknowledge the work of cinema as a specific form of expression and put to work the viewer herself. Godard did not want the viewer to be lost in the film or have the film lost on the viewer. He wanted attention of a different kind, an alert, inquisitive viewer, who could keep up with the filmmaker's own intelligence, allusiveness, and politics. Godard's politics developed leftward over the course of his enormous output (sometimes two films a year) in the 1960s. His early films, about gangsters (*Breathless*, 1959), about gender and how it is understood on screen (*My Life to Live*, 1962), and about how moviemaking could be used to interrogate the politics of representation (*Contempt*, 1963), are about how we see and interpret what we see on the screen. As the Vietnam War raged and protests grew around the world, Godard slowly but surely embraced an ideology of Marxism-Maoism, a radical politics of revolution. In the end, by the late 1960s, his politics would move him away from making fiction films and into agitprop—complex films that propounded his ideology. But before that happened, the inquisitiveness that marked his early work grew more extreme. His impatience with traditional cinematic storytelling devices was more marked. This all came to a head in his 1967 film about the end of the bourgeois world, *Weekend* (from the popular French word for weekend, *le weekend*).

French writers and filmmakers, themselves members of the middle class, have traditionally taken aim at this class, attacking it for its complacency, its acquisitiveness, its fake moralism and dubious moral authority. None went as far as Godard to see the end of the bourgeois world in violent, apocalyptic terms. *Weekend* begins with a warning in bold, red letters, roughly translated as "Prohibited for viewers under 18." It is followed by a few more curious titles: "A Film Adrift in the Cosmos." The action begins with a couple finishing drinks on a balcony and suggesting the murder of the woman's family in a car accident. Then another title: "A Film Found in a Dump." The cosmos and a dump. Lost and found. Universality and trash. Godard can't quite make up his mind. What he is certain about is that the film will not leave us be; it will continue to provoke us, to interrupt our and its own line of thought. Or conversely, interruption *is* the film's line of thought. Godard is practicing the politics of disruption and interruption. And excess, a movie about unrest made to cause unrest, a puzzle and a cry for change—in the cosmos and the dump.

And on the road. *Weekend* (the film's title is finally spelled out multiple times across the screen in the red, white, and blue of the French flag) is a road movie. And we get a hint of this early on, when Corinne (the woman on the balcony, played by Mireille Darc) looks down to see men fighting over a near accident. The fight escalates and the music becomes more ominous. But there is no real plotline developing here or throughout the film, other than Corinne and her husband, Roland (Jean Yanne), taking to the road to kill her parents for her father's money. The opening sequence, hinting at infidelity and murderous provocations, leads not to a plot, but to a prolonged sequence, shot in a single take and with the characters almost in silhouette, in which Corinne, sitting on a table in bra and panties, tells a pornographic story about a sexual encounter. The ominous music continues, sometimes overwhelming the dialogue, and Godard interrupts her story with a graphic, an unsavory pun in French or English:

ANAL

YSE

Godard loves puns because he loves the intricacies and ironies of language—spoken and written as well as cinematic. In language—verbal and visual—is power, to see, to interpret, to analyze. Language can reveal or mask, can be plain or complex. Godard loves complexity. The provocative tale spun by Corinne (she admits she doesn't know if it is true or a nightmare) is about excess, the inability to be sexually satisfied. This cuts two ways. The characters in *Weekend*, "real," mythical, or imaginary, are excessive in their needs and desires. They want so much that they wind up eating each other. The film *Weekend* is excessive cinema. It tells too much, its complexity is too much, its vision of a world devouring itself is too much. A car wreck of a movie. "The road of excess leads to the palace of wisdom," wrote the poet William Blake. We can get swallowed in *Weekend*'s excess unless we analyze, an activity that might lead to wisdom.

Corinne and her husband Roland's road trip starts with a contretemps; the couple engage in spray painting and a shooting over a fender bender. "Scene of Parisian Life," reads the title. The couple heads out for the road. It is important to note here that the road movie is a venerable form, almost a genre in itself, at least in American cinema. It follows upon an older literary genre, the *bildungsroman*, where a young man travels the road, learning hard lessons along the way. In cinema, the road movie can be a comedy, as in Frank Capra's *It Happened One Night* (1934), or about an outlaw couple on the run, as in Arthur Penn's *Bonnie and Clyde* (1967), itself a film with many antecedents in the history of film. (Before Penn came onboard, Godard was invited to be the director of *Bonnie and Clyde*.) There is an irony here. The film bases itself on a venerable Hollywood convention, but subverts that convention at every turn of the road. In Godard's hands, the road movie becomes a trip into a kind of parallel universe, full of imaginary beings, of garbage men spouting Marxist theory, and, finally, bands of guerillas at the end of the bourgeois universe.

But not before Godard creates cinema's longest traffic jam (Figure 7.1). For eight minutes, Godard's camera tracks a line of cars (at one point you can see the camera and crew reflected in a car's window) stuck on a country road. Showing absurd patience, people toss a ball from one car to another. Men play cards and chess; one unfurls the sails of his boat. There's a zoo caravan with lions and monkeys. A gigantic gas truck. There are overturned cars and, at the end, carnage with blood (or, as Godard would say, "not blood, red"[3]) and torn bodies strewn around the road. Corinne and Roland, of course, jump the queue, driving in the opposite lane, race past the road-kill and continue on their way. But their way leads them further into a heart of darkness, though this will not be Joseph Conrad's darkness. There is no madman deep in the forest, but there is craziness there; the madness is in the class represented by the two protagonists. Among all the other things it is, *Weekend* is a satire, an exaggeration of the worst traits of a class, a tale of excess and its discontents, of the end of a suffocating ideology at the hands of a voracious one.

Another pun:

FAUX

"False Photograph/Photography." What you see is not what you think you see; maybe not even what you see—after all, this is just an image on the screen. This particular graphic is inserted at the end of a sequence in which Corinne and Roland get involved, or more accurately refuse to get involved, with a Marxist farmer, whose tractor collides with a fancy sports car, killing one of its occupants. More blood, more red. The dead man's companion rails against the farmer, but, in the face of Corinne and Roland driving off without giving assistance, winds up embracing him as others look on, laughing. A "photograph" of the farmer, the woman from the crash, and our scowling Roland, among other onlookers, follows the graphic. The *Internationale*—the Communist international anthem—plays underneath the image. False photography indeed. Godard is broadly insisting that class struggle is more than the brief, bloody encounter of farmer and rich person, or perhaps that's where it might start. He is teasing his viewers with an image that is culturally, sociologically improbable. A fragment adrift in the cosmos; Marx on the road where opposites meet to destroy each other.

With the image and the graphic, Godard has halted the film for a moment to make a number of points about basic Marxist principles. He has reduced those principles to something approaching comedy: we may or may not take what we have seen seriously—can class struggle be reduced to a fight between a farmer and a couple in a sports car?

Figure 7.1 Weekend: the traffic jam.

88 Politics and the apocalypse

Can the participants and antagonists suddenly join in brotherhood and sisterhood? But what Godard is very serious about is the complexity of image-making and his ability to be didactic and ironic, even comedic, simultaneously, to look at radical politics almost as if through the lens of a comic book, while at the same time calling upon history, literature, and cinema.

Corinne and Roland continue on their road trip into the heart of violence, assaulted by other drivers, and taken at gunpoint by a mad couple, the man identifying himself as Joseph Balsamo, an 18th-century figure of mystery and intrigue and the subject of books by the French author Alexandre Dumas. Never content with historical and literary allusion, Godard flashes a title: *The Exterminating Angel*, a bizarre film made in 1962 by the great Spanish surrealist, Luis Buñuel, about a group of bourgeoisie who cannot escape from a dinner party. Joseph holds Corinne and Roland hostage in their car. He proclaims himself God and announces the start of a cinema of flamboyance, which is, of course, represented by the film we are seeing. When our couple do gain the upper hand, chasing Joseph and his companion, Marie Madeleine, into a field of wrecked cars, Joseph raises his arms and creates a miracle. A great flock of sheep appear—as they do in Buñuel's film. We are now through the looking glass. Nothing is real, nothing is false, and Roland and Corinne wander through a fiery wreck (Figure 7.2). They are now on foot.

Time becomes malleable; characters changeable. The film wanders between intersecting worlds—the past of the French Revolution and

Figure 7.2 Automobile apocalypse.

the future of an apocalypse of car wrecks and latter-day, or perhaps post-apocalyptic, revolutionaries. Jean-Pierre Léaud, a stalwart actor of the French New Wave, suddenly appears in 17th-century costume, quoting from the French revolutionary figure Saint-Just. Then, just as suddenly, he is in street clothes, singing a song in a telephone booth as Corinne and Roland attempt to steal his car. They continue to wander through the countryside. They meet Emily Brontë and her oddly dressed companion, quoting Bertolt Brecht. "What a rotten film," says Roland, perhaps echoing the viewer's sentiments; "all we meet are crazy people." They set fire to Emily. They steal clothes from the corpses strewn around car wrecks. They are picked up by an itinerant pianist, who sets up in a farmyard and plays Mozart, which allows Godard to create a musical interlude, during which his camera does what may be the most unusual movement disallowed by the rules of film: a 360-degree pan and track completely circling the farm—not once, but twice, before changing and repeating it in the opposite direction.

Godard is doing a number of things to the picture plane—that surface on which his images appear. He is calling attention to it, to the devices available to him, like creating the traffic jam or the circular pan and track around the barnyard, to the spectacle of wrecked cars and bloodied corpses, to people asking if they are in a film or reality. He is using it to create historical and political depth, calling forth the French Revolution and imagining a revolution to come that will (literally) eat away at the complacent violence of the bored middle class. He's using it to test our patience and to preach. After Roland allows Corinne to be raped by a passing stranger, they are picked up by a garbage truck, whose garbage men—one a dark-skinned African, the other an Algerian—deliver a very long speech about capitalism, imperialism, Fascism, racism, and the Revolution, words borrowed from Marx, Engels, Frantz Fanon, and Stokely Carmichael.[4] Each of the garbage men speaks for the other, and Godard focuses on the person not speaking, so that we see one eating his lunch and hear the other talk. Interspersed are various scenes from earlier in the film. Recall the opening title? "A Film Found in a Dump." Here are the fragments gathered by the garbage men in their disquisition about oppression and revolution. The weight of all the absurd incidents in the film falls on their long, didactic speeches of Marxist doctrine. It is an act of collection, of placing all the disparate elements and events of the film in the context of ideological doctrine. The garbage men reign in the film's apparent nonsense with voices of authority. Fauxtographie.

When *Weekend* first appeared, many people took issue with the garbage men's speech: it is relentless and boring, and it stopped short the antic surrealism of the film. But it is also Godard practicing Brechtian theory. Stop the action and talk directly to the audience about political fact and theory. Irritate the audience if necessary, but make a point, make a film politically as well as about politics. Alter the viewer's notion of cinematic reality. Which is what happens when the garbage men have finished their lunch and their speech, part of which is dedicated to the theory of the formation of primitive tribes. In a flash forward, we get our first glimpse of a tribe, a group of garishly dressed hippies. But first, Corinne and Roland carry out their task of killing Corinne's mother, stabbing her as the image of a red-soaked skinned rabbit takes the place of the murder itself.

Enter the FLSO, the *Front de Liberation de Seine et Oise*, the Seine and Oise Liberation Front. The graphic that announces this, in the red, white, and blue of the French flag, has a big white "X" across it, as if Godard were canceling out his own creation, indicating its imaginary existence, or laughing at its impossibility. The guerillas use walkie-talkies to communicate with each other and their code names are movie titles: *Battleship Potemkin* and *The Searchers*. They live in the forest to the steady rhythm of drums and poetry. But there is nothing attractive about them. The FLSO are sexual torturers, murderers—they stab Roland to death—and cannibals. They serve him up with the tourists they shot earlier. "The horror of the Bourgeoisie can only be overcome by more horror," one of them announces. This echoes lines from Bertolt Brecht's poem, "To Posterity": "Alas, we / who wished to lay the foundations for kindness / Could not ourselves be kind."[5] A rugged revolutionary statement, but one that, in Godard's hands, only proclaims violence as an end—something Godard emphasizes not only with the simulated death and disembowelment of Roland, but the actual slaughter of farm animals. This is unpleasant to watch, but it's necessary to underscore Godard's own ambivalence about what he is creating. The garbage men's speeches were theory only. Now Godard creates a group of revolutionaries who are putting theory into violent practice.

"Faux Raccord" announces a title card in the midst of the violence and the death of one of the guerillas. "False Connection." Between what? Between theory and practice? Between the death of one of the female FLSO members, who sings a tender song as she dies, and the cannibalism practiced by her tribe? Between Godard's own imaginative flights and the need for radical action? Is there, finally, no possible connection between radical political cinema and radical political action? That is a probable reading, given the end of the film. Corinne enjoys the stew of tourist mixed in with her husband prepared by the

Politics and the apocalypse 91

blood-soaked chef, Ernest, and she asks for more (Figure 7.3). "Fin" announces the end title. "End." But not quite; it goes on:

FIN DE CONTE

FIN DE CINEMA

End of story. End of cinema. But whose cinema? Movies went on to be made after *Weekend*. Is Godard then announcing the end of *his* cinema of the 1960s which itself revolutionized cinema worldwide? Godard continued to make movies, but for a long time they were less narrative fictions and more political agitprops. He then moved to video and digital production and now, in his eighties, is still making films, though without the fire of creativity that marked his earlier work. *Weekend* is, perhaps, the end of politically *polite* cinema, the end of what conventional movies can get away with, even though they continue to get away with it. The end of the cinema of entertainment and escape.

These days, we have no end of apocalyptic and post-apocalyptic movies. Zombies lurch; the land is desolate. People wander a broken world. Many such films reflect a real fear of what climate change and political unrest might lead to. They are films of anxiety as opposed to *Weekend*, which is a film of satirical delight in its own exploits and that looks at the end of the world with a kind of malicious glee.

Figure 7.3 End of cinema: serving up a meal of some tourist and Corinne's husband.

The film, like Stanley Kubrick's 1964 *Dr. Strangelove or: How I Learned to Stop Worrying and Love the Bomb* (which we will look at in a later chapter), is a deadly serious joke and a bit prophetic. France would come close to revolution just a year after Godard's film. There was no cannibalism and an aroused middle class ended the students' and workers' uprising. And the energy of the New Wave dissipated. Revolution failed.

Notes

1 Quoted by J. Hoberman, www.criterion.com/current/posts/356-tout-va-bien-revisited.
2 Godard calls for starting from zero in his 1968 film, *Le gai savoir*.
3 "Let's Talk about *Pierrot*: An Interview with Jean-Luc Godard," http://a-bittersweet-life.tumblr.com/post/4220398026/lets-talk-about-pierrot-an-interview-with.
4 See Daniel Fairfax, "End of Story, End of Cinema: *Weekend* (Jean-Luc Godard, 1967)," *Senses of Cinema* (March 2017), http://sensesofcinema.com/2017/1967/weekend-jean-luc-godard-1967.
5 Trans. H. R. Hays, www.poemhunter.com/poem/to-posterity.

Further reading

Richard Brody, *Everything is Cinema: The Working Life of Jean-Luc Godard* (New York: Metropolitan Books, 2008).
Sylvia Harvey, *May '68 and Film Culture* (London: BFI Publishing, 1980).
Tom Milne, ed. and trans., *Godard on Godard* (New York: Da Capo Press, 1986).
James Monaco, *The New Wave: Truffaut, Godard, Chabrol, Rohmer, Rivette* (Sag Harbor, NY: Harbor Electronic Publishing, 2004).
Richard Neupert, *A History of the French New Wave Cinema* (Madison, WI: University of Wisconsin Press, 2002).
John Willett, ed. and trans., *Brecht on Theatre: The Development of an Aesthetic* (New York: Hill and Wang, 1992).

8 Reflections on Fascism
The Conformist (1970)

All artistic movements, just like the cultures that give them life, have a period of ascendance and descent. They flourish and then die out. Sometimes they are revived, as modernism was in the filmmaking of the 1960s and 70s. In their descent, they will bleed into newer movements, lending their influence, being revived in different forms. The surrealist and Dada movements early in the 20th century—movements that mocked high art and reveled in absurdity—became part of the modernist movement in the visual arts and moved into avant-garde cinema. Political movements also have a lifespan, though these tend to be longer than artistic ones. There was a measure of democracy in some European countries before and immediately after WWI. The mindless destruction wrought by that war, the economic inflation, the cultural depression, the political unrest, rampant anti-Semitism, and nationalism led, in Italy and then in Germany, to Fascism.

Benito Mussolini, Italy's fascist leader, started his political career as a revolutionary socialist. But his preening, narcissistic personality was drawn to the dictatorial possibilities of a new Roman empire and he strong-armed his way to power by forming a gang of "black-shirt" thugs, who marched on Rome and effectively took over the government in 1922. Mussolini governed by force and the promise to make Italy great again. He conquered Ethiopia; he practiced anti-Semitism in a country where hatred of Jews was not the norm. He became Hitler's comrade in the attempted destruction of Europe and its Jews. When the war was all but over in 1945, his followers turned on him, killed him, and hung him upside down in the town square.[1]

There was an artistic movement associated with Italian Fascism called futurism. Unlike the return to the old-fashioned heroic art favored by the Germans (who attempted to destroy all modernist works they claimed were "degenerate"), or the socialist realism of the USSR that favored heroic poses by peasants and workers, futurism made use of the abstract forms and bold colors of contemporary modernist painting and sculpture. It was a loud, jagged, violent art, supported by the theories behind the movement, voiced by the painter Marinetti. In his *Futurist Manifesto*, he wrote:

> We will glorify war—the world's only hygiene—militarism, patriotism, the destructive gesture of freedom-bringers, beautiful ideas worth dying for, and scorn for woman.
> We will destroy the museums, libraries, academies of every kind, will fight moralism, feminism, every opportunistic or utilitarian cowardice.[2]

Such brutality of thought reflected and tainted the movement. It was a statement of politics masquerading as aesthetics and aesthetics glorifying war. It could be applied, with little modification, to the Nazi movement in Germany glorified by Leni Riefenstahl in *Triumph of the Will*.

After the war, with Italy in ruins, neorealism became the dominant aesthetic, and the differences in intent and execution are important. The futurist aggression toward all things humane is reversed in neorealism, whose focus is on the most vulnerable members of a devastated country. As narrative film, neorealism eschews abstraction, focusing instead on an almost documentary gaze at the streets of Rome or the poor fishing villages in the countryside. Its characters are quietly desperate; their stories are of loss and struggle. Its images aren't harsh; they are true to the streets through which their characters wander. Character and place appear to embrace each other. Neorealism was not exactly a modernist form. There are aspects of it that are quite traditional. But it is an intensely political form, focusing on working-class people in an inhospitable country.

As I noted in Chapter 5, out of neorealism came a revitalization of cinema not only in Italy but the world over. In Italy itself there was a transition that occurred among the original neorealist directors. Federico Fellini, Luchino Visconti, Michelangelo Antonioni, and Pier Paolo Pasolini moved on from their neorealist roots to embrace modernist forms. Antonioni especially became a filmmaker who turned the neorealist aesthetic into an almost painterly study of figures in a landscape, lost, aching, diminished by the world around them. Films like *L'avventura* (1960), *Red Desert* (1964), and *Blow-Up* (1966) are remarkable visions of physical things impinging and infiltrating the lives of humans stuck in existential crises.

Bernardo Bertolucci was of the next generation, and the youngest of Italian filmmakers following upon the neorealist movement. His early films began extending and expanding on the premises of neorealism, but with a left-wing political edge and a cinematic style that came under the influence of Jean-Luc Godard. He moved beyond Godard, developing, with his cinematographer Vittorio Storaro, a lush, sweeping, lyrical style, full of color and generous in its camera movements. The films of his early mature period—*The Spider's Stratagem* (1970), *The Conformist* (1970), and *Last Tango in Paris* (1972)—are marked by an eye eager to explore the spaces around his characters and the objects that surround them. His is a cinema of things, of careful creation and examination of the details of the cinematic worlds he creates. And these films are political, but in a very different way than Godard's. *The Conformist*, the film we will explore here, examines Italian Fascism and attempts to explain it as a kind of hallucination of a man insecure in his very presence in the world, in his sense of himself as a man of action, in his own sexuality; so insecure that he joins the fascist cause to prove that he is a heterosexual man of action, even if it involves the violent destruction of others.

The Conformist is a cinematic contradiction. Its subject is a simultaneously attractive and sordid individual who chooses to take part in a vile regime. Its formal structure is lush and dramatic, full of startling compositions and audacious editing. The camera is fluid and the musical score by Georges Delerue is almost nostalgic in its elegant sweep. Its unhappy protagonist is played by Jean-Louis Trintignant, among the most impressive actors of the 1960s and 70s French and Italian cinema. As we analyze the film, we need to keep questioning its contradictions—is it an anti-fascist film or does it indulge in nostalgia for the very period it despises? In what ways is it a political film made politically?

Bertolucci solves the problem by creating a metaphor that encompasses the film: blindness and seeing; illusion vs. reality. He foregrounds this metaphor by reaching back to classic Greek philosophy, and Plato's myth of the cave: a group of prisoners are chained together in a cave, forced to look at the wall in front of them. Behind them are their captors who parade puppets in front of a fire, so that the shadows are cast on that wall. The prisoners are allowed only to look at the shadows. The meaning of Plato's story is that what we see are the mere reflections of things, not the things themselves. The reality of things, of life itself, is hidden in a veil of illusion. It's a bit like cinema itself, where we watch the shadows of images imprinted on a sheet of film or stored as digital code and projected from behind us on to a screen in front of us or formed by LED crystals on a TV flatscreen. Cinema always denies us the real thing, no matter how real the thing appears to be. *The Conformist* tells of a man who believes the things he believes he has seen; believes in a strange story of his past; believes

96 Reflections on Fascism

in the mirage of Fascism. Marcello Clerici, the film's conformist, lives in the shadows of his own fears and cowardice, and he acts on them in a continual motion of bad faith.

While Plato's myth of the cave saturates the whole of *The Conformist*, Bertolucci retells it in full when Clerici visits his old left-wing professor, named Quadri, a man the fascists have ordered him to assassinate. The scene occurs near the middle of the film, at its core. As Clerici repeats Plato's story for his professor, the shadows in the room keep changing, as if the film's visuals themselves were telling the tale. Clerici darkens the room so that the only light comes from one open window, casting his own shadow on the wall, placing the professor in silhouette. The camera is low and tilted, placing the whole scene off kilter. Clerici moves in and out of the light, at one point giving the fascist salute, at another confronting his own shadow on the wall (Figure 8.1). The shadows keep shifting as the two square off in an attempt to find the light. Quadri tells him that in fascist Italy the people are Plato's prisoners confusing shadows for reality. He is talking about Clerici as well, a man of confused motives and a shocking lack of self-knowledge, a man whose personality is in the shadows. Quadri tells Clerici that a real fascist would not say the things he has said, would not be as intelligent and open to argument. He opens the window and Clerici's shadow disappears. Clerici is a fake, a man living in bad faith without insight or self-knowledge. Quadri sadly misjudges him.

Figure 8.1 The Conformist: Marcello Clerici (Jean-Louis Trintignant) gives the fascist salute while recounting Plato's myth of the cave in the shadows of his professor's room.

Like *Weekend*, *The Conformist* is a road movie of sorts. Clerici is being driven to his rendezvous with the professor in order to assassinate him. His driver is his fascist minder, Manganiello (he is named after the *manganello*, the club that fascist thugs used to beat their victims). During the drive, Bertolucci pieces together in a nonlinear structure the moments real and imagined of Clerici's past, the events that led to his becoming a fascist. I say "imagined" because many of these moments are so surreal that they defy the codes of cinematic realism. They are the memories of a man basing his politics, indeed his existence, on a childhood incident in which he believes (and we see) that he shot his chauffeur, Lino, who was making sexual advances in a building fluttering with white sheets. The story is actually a double flashback. Clerici walks beside Manganiello's car in a bleak winter landscape. This triggers images of the thirteen-year-old Clerici being molested by his classmates and escaping by jumping into the car of his chauffeur. This in turn cuts to the adult Marcello confessing the story to his priest—all too eager to hear the details—of the incident of seduction and murder, which we then witness. If true, Clerici is suffering from a childhood trauma; if not, his search for a "normal" life is based on a lie. For the adult Clerici it means a search for an ordinary life of ordinary sexuality and membership in an extraordinary regime that hunts down "subversives." He compensates for his past—real or imagined—by becoming a would-be assassin in the present.

Memories, true or false, are nested within memories; within, perhaps, dreams. Earlier, Clerici recalls his meeting with a fascist official at a darkened radio studio, where his blind friend Italo is delivering a speech about the axis of Italy and Germany—the wartime alliance of fascist powers. The two are seen in reflections through the studio glass—images and shadows. Clerici falls asleep and awakens with a start to see a fascist bigwig telling him to go to the Minister's office to receive his orders. His interview is intercut with the visit to that office, a gigantic open space with a large desk in the middle. Vast halls and looming shadows, disorienting and overwhelming. In the outside hall, men pass by carrying statues, like the guards in Plato's myth. The disorientation grows as the film progresses. When Clerici enters the Minister's office, he sees a woman spread out on the desk. He will meet this woman (played by Dominique Sanda), in different guises, three times in the course of the film: here on the desk, later as a slightly mad prostitute as he stops on his way to Paris to assassinate his professor, and finally as the professor's seductive wife.

Is this a hallucination? Are we seeing the entire film through the filter of Clerici's undependable memory and bad conscience? Anna, the professor's wife, tries her best to save her husband. She attempts to seduce Clerici *and* Clerici's wife, using her ambient sexuality to no avail, but to such effect that it infuses Clerici's recall. She becomes for him (and the viewer) a kind of everywoman, seen multiple times in multiple guises, whose double is Clerici's wife, a pretty, middle-class girl (played by Stefania Sandrelli), who Clerici marries to prove that he is normal. Anna is the dream of a more provocative woman, and she will die for her attempts to save her husband.

Understanding this, we get a clue to Bertolucci's strategy in *The Conformist*. The quest for normality that so obsesses Clerici is countered by the strange situations he finds himself in and, more importantly, the unusual visual and narrative construction that tells his story, which is as hallucinatory as it is "real." Early in the film, Clerici directs Manganiello to go to his mother's house. The camera all but deliriously sweeps across the dead leaves blowing across the driveway and, inside the house, where Clerici finds a heroin syringe under his mother's bed (a bed covered with puppies), the camera moves in defiance of architecture by tracking past a wall in one direction and then, reversing the position of the shot, tracks back in the opposite direction. No part of Clerici's life is normal, and this is reflected in the things Bertolucci's camera sees and the ways he sees them. We understand this stunningly when he and his mother visit his father in an asylum, glaringly white save for the black straightjacket worn by the father. He was a committed fascist, who is now literally committed. He forced castor oil on prisoners (a favorite humiliation delivered to political prisoners by the Italians); he tortured and murdered—and now he can do little more than repeat the phrase "Slaughter and melancholy" (Figure 8.2). This is Clerici's inheritance, and it's what he wants to slip back into, to become a fascist like his father before him and, perhaps, go mad.

The notion of Clerici as an empty vessel is important to our understanding of the film and its politics. Bertolucci wants to create a character without a moral center, but who *thinks* that morality means normality and believes that normality is being a fascist, which is of course not normal at all. Despite the charisma of actor Jean-Louis Trintignant, or perhaps because of it, we are asked to see Clerici as a pathetic character, but, finally, as a coward. He is unable to assassinate Professor Quadri and his wife. He sits impassively in the car as Anna pounds on the window, begging for her life, and Quadri is stabbed repeatedly in the snow by a gang of black-shirts. Anna herself is shot to death while running through the woods, attempting to escape.

Reflections on Fascism 99

Figure 8.2 "Slaughter and melancholy": Clerici visits his father, a fascist now confined in an asylum.

There is a cut after the scene of slaughter, and the film brings us to 1943. Italy has surrendered and Mussolini has resigned (soon to be killed by his own people). A heavier, older Clerici lives in the darkened straits of a wartime apartment with his wife, child, and other tenants. A radio announces the latest news. The scene has the air of a neorealist film. Clerici goes outside to meet his blind friend Italo and to see, he says, a dictator fall. Crowds mill about; a group pulls the broken head of a Mussolini statue from the back of a motorbike. Clerici has Italo remove his fascist badge. And suddenly he sees Lino, the chauffeur, the man who presumably awakened Clerici's latent homosexuality that worried him to become a "normal" fascist, the man he supposedly killed. Lino, now old and balding, is seducing a young man who lives on the streets, eating cats and rats to survive. Clerici gets hysterical, blaming Lino for the death of Quadri and his wife. He yells "Assassin," and in his madness, loudly denounces Italo. A group of marchers celebrating the liberation surrounds them, the second time Clerici has been swallowed by a crowd. The first was in a dance hall where Anna and Clerici's wife danced together and then drew everyone into a circle, creating a vortex around Clerici.

Now Clerici is trapped in the vortex of his own bad faith and bad conscience, desperately trying to hurl out the blame that he cannot absorb into himself. The crowd sweeps Italo away and leaves Clerici sitting by a fire, looking through a gate at the gay street-person, like a prisoner in Plato's cave, still unable to tell reality from its shadow (Figure 8.3).

Bertolucci has created an extraordinary tale of self-delusion and political terrorism. The film poses important questions about why an individual might join an abhorrent regime and how such a regime depends on weak, gullible individuals to buy into its lies and brutalities. The political right plays upon people's desires for strength and an illusory individuality, on their fears and resentments, on their felt need to be part of a large-scale empowering movement. Such politics fill a lack—of something missing from their lives, or a perceived injustice—and too often are based on the hatred of minority groups. Marcello Clerici, in *The Conformist*, fears an insufficiency of "normal" masculinity and tries to purchase it from the fascist apparatus. But it is an illusion, and hence the hallucinatory elements of the film. It is blindness, and hence the play on light and shadow. Clerici is not so much a prisoner in Plato's cave as he is a prisoner of his own self-delusion. And perhaps that is the same thing.

Earlier I asked whether the visual energy of *The Conformist* works against its anti-fascist content. In retrospect we can understand that form and content here play a kind of counterpoint with each other. The seductiveness of Bertolucci's images speaks to the seduction Fascism holds for the film's central character—perhaps all characters in life itself who fall under the spell of right-wing brutality. At the

Figure 8.3 Clerici looks back at his own false memories at the end of *The Conformist*.

same time, they are made not to seduce us, the film's viewers, but to engage us in the swirl of events created by a man who is diminished by the world in which we see him. The images are powerful enough to create a kind of distance: we watch, are moved, and at the same time we understand who this pathetic individual is. He is less than the sum of the world he blindly attempts to navigate.

Bertolucci went on to make another extraordinary film, *Last Tango in Paris* (1972), a scandal in its time because of its overt sexuality. But *Last Tango* is also a political film, this time about the politics of intimacy and self-destruction. The film contains an intense performance by Marlon Brando, one of the great American actors, and it is even more visually seductive than *The Conformist*. The subsequent films of Bertolucci's career never matched the power of the three potent works of his early period, which stand as visually extraordinary examples of political cinema. To be sure, *The Last Emperor* (1987), an "epic" about China from the turn of the 20th century to the early 1960s, swept the Oscars for that year. But this and Bertolucci's subsequent films lack the formal and political intensity of *The Spider's Stratagem*, *The Conformist*, and *Last Tango in Paris*. This falling off occasionally occurs to artists in any medium, and our focus should remain on the films that best represent the artist's imaginative vigor. *The Conformist*'s intensity of insight into an aspect of the fascist mind is unique, as is its delirious visual style. It is an important example of the vitality of political cinema during the 1960s and 70s.

Notes

1 For a history of Italian Fascism see, for example, www.slate.com/articles/news_and_politics/fascism/2017/01/how_italian_fascists_succeeded_in_taking_over_italy.html.
2 The full manifesto is at www.italianfuturism.org/manifestos/foundingmanifesto.

Further reading

Fabian Gerard, T. Jefferson Kline, Bruce Sklarew, eds., *Berolucci: Interviews* (Oxford, MS: University of Mississippi Press, 2000).
Robert Phillip Kolker, *Bertolucci* (London: The British Film Institute, 1985).
Claretta Tonetti, *Bernardo Bertolucci: The Cinema of Ambiguity* (Woodbridge, CT: Twayne Publisher, 2005).

9 The Cold War, part one
Science fiction and *Invasion of the Body Snatchers* (1956)

From the flourishing of political cinema in Europe and beyond, we return to the United States and move back a bit in time, to the 1950s and the prolonged period of political repression known as the Cold War. I use the word "repression" carefully. Unlike the physical repression occurring in the Soviet Union—the country the United States saw as the great enemy from the late 1940s to the late 1980s—where enemies real and imagined were imprisoned and shot, repression in the United States took more subtle forms. People were imprisoned, and two of them, Ethel and Julius Rosenberg, were electrocuted for passing secrets to the Russians. But the major effect was economic—people lost their jobs for being accused of Communism—cultural, in the form of a pall over the freedom of thought in the United States, and political, in the rise of right-wing demagogues who built fame and occasionally fortune riding the wave of anti-Communism.

To understand this, we need to gather up some history. The end of WWII in 1945 brought little relief to global anxieties. The growing revelation of Nazi atrocities, and the full scope of the attempted extermination of the Jews, left people helpless in an attempt to understand the depths of depravity into which a civilized country might fall. The death of Franklin Delano Roosevelt after twelve years as President left a gaping hole in the country's political culture. The Soviet Union, not only U.S. allies during the war, but the nation that lost millions of citizens in its fight to defeat Nazi Germany, became the enemy. Not merely the enemy, but a mythical force of evil—very much of the West's own making, aided by Stalin's crimes—that, we were told, insinuated itself into every aspect of American life and threatened to take over the world.

It needn't have been that way. Russia came out of the war devastated. There were some 20,000,000 military and civilian deaths with 25,000,000 left homeless. This compared to 400,000 military and no domestic civilian deaths for the United States, and 338,000 military and civilian deaths in the United Kingdom.[1] Entire Russian villages were in ruins; Leningrad (now St. Petersburg) was nearly destroyed. Franklin Delano Roosevelt was on relatively good terms—as good as possible—with the Soviet dictator Joseph Stalin. But Stalin wanted a great deal in return for Russia's sacrifices: he wanted control of many of the lands, like Poland and what became East Germany, that Russia liberated from the Nazis. He blockaded Berlin and the U.S. responded with an airlift of food to keep the city going until it was eventually divided into four zones: Russian, British, French, and U.S. All of these actions, along with Stalin's expansionist desires and his bloodthirsty liquidation of his alleged enemies, solidified the image of an implacable foe.

Roosevelt's successor, Harry Truman, had less patience with Stalin than his predecessor, and, insecure in Roosevelt's shadow, felt it necessary to stand up to Stalin. In collaboration with Congress, which shifted back and forth between Republican and Democratic majorities after the war, Truman initiated programs and policies that started the Cold War, instituting it as political and cultural policy for decades to come. He established the Truman Doctrine and the Marshall Plan. The first, announced in 1947, pledged the U.S. to defend countries from Soviet aggression. It was prompted by a major Cold War document, the so-called "long telegram" by George Kennan, advising that Soviet expansionism should be contained wherever it occurred. The Marshall Plan poured money into Europe to counter Soviet expansion and the strength of national Communist parties. By 1949, Russia had recovered enough from the war to build and test an atomic bomb. It was slowly regaining its military might, further frightening the West. To add to the fears, the Korean War broke out in in 1950. But perhaps the most insidious event of the postwar world, at least as it influenced the internal affairs and culture of the United States, was Truman's 1947 institution of a "loyalty oath" for federal employees, making them swear they were not Communists. The fact was there were few Communists in the U.S., inside the government or in the population at large. At its peak, in 1938, the Communist party of the United States had some 100,000 members, and their "subversive acts" were mostly aimed at agitation for civil rights and other progressive causes. Some were spies. When Stalin and Hitler signed a non-aggression pact in 1939, there was a rapid loss in membership over what appeared to be a sellout of Russia to a Nazi regime. In short, there was never a "Communist threat" in the United States, but this reality had no effect on growing anti-Communist hysteria.

The combination of Russian military and economic muscle combined with the fear that somehow Communism would infiltrate the American system of government and the very thoughts of the country's citizens provided a potent mix for exploitation and fear. 1950 was a crucial year. Alger Hiss, a State Department official, hounded by Richard Nixon, former Communist Whittaker Chambers, and the House Committee on Un-American Activities (HUAC), was convicted of perjury in connection with his spying for the Soviet Union. In February that year, Senator Joseph McCarthy made a speech in Wheeling, West Virginia. He pulled a piece of paper out of his pocket and stated that it contained the names of 205 State Department officials who were Communists. The number kept changing every time McCarthy made the speech, and he never found any Communists, anywhere. But that didn't matter; what he did find was a cultural-political anxiety and weakness to exploit, and it catapulted him into infamy. He and his Senate committee gained extraordinary power based on lies and intimidation, and ruined many lives with false accusations that a gullible public took as the truth.

That still wasn't the end of it. Ethel and Julius Rosenberg were accused by a relative of being Communist spies, passing atomic secrets to the Soviet Union. Though there was no proof at the time (subsequently it appears likely that Julius was a spy), they were tried and in 1953 executed. Spying was (and still is) an international occupation among governments. During the Cold War, fear of spies became part of the general cultural paranoia, and the politics of discovering and naming spies, "fellow travelers," and "fifth amendment Communists" was an occupation that made political careers for some and destroyed the lives of others—quite literally in the case of the Rosenbergs. The author Lillian Hellman called the period "scoundrel time."

As I noted, anti-Communism was not merely a political and military preoccupation of the Cold War; it became a cultural preoccupation as well. The CIA set up groups of anti-Communist artists and intellectuals to spread the word about American exceptionalism and Communist perfidy at home and abroad.[2] Any progressive ideas, any ideas at all that were somewhat left of center, were condemned as Communist. Anti-Communism became a threat and an ideological straitjacket. Children were instructed to "duck and cover" under their school desks as practice against a Russian nuclear attack. Neighbors joked to neighbors, "I hear McCarthy is coming after you." Sometimes he was.

Movies responded to the Cold War in a variety of ways. Often they ignored it, as much as possible. The politics of containment, of keeping the Russians from expanding their power, was transferred into films about constrained, contained lives. Alfred Hitchcock's *Rear Window* (1954) is such a film. While avoiding overt mention of politics, with its portrait of a man confined to a wheelchair, passing his time by spying on his neighbors with a telephoto lens, the film comes close to an allegory of the moment, transferring geopolitical containment into the body of a contained individual: reduced, all but impotent, able only to live through others. There were films during the Cold War that addressed Cold War politics directly. Some of them toed the anti-Communist line, like the hysteria-ridden *My Son John* (Leo McCarey, 1952) in which a mother all but loses her mind when her son comes out as a Communist. Some glorified the hunt for "Reds" like the John Wayne vehicle, *Big Jim McLain* (1952).

Among the most popular genres of the 1950s was science fiction. There are a number of reasons for this. The use of the atomic bomb to wipe out two Japanese cities at the end of WWII frightened people about the nuclear power. The images of the destroyed cities along with the newsreels of nuclear tests were terrifying examples of science as a destructive force. Then there were sightings of flying saucers. These began in 1947, a few years after the war and the dropping of the bomb, and during the uptick of investigations by the HUAC. Among the most intriguing of the sightings was the claim that a saucer crash-landed near a military base in Roswell, New Mexico. Some people believed that we were being invaded by aliens from outer space.

But consider this: people were afraid of the destructive potential of science while right-wing politicians were telling them that they were under threat of an alien (read "Communist") ideology, even an alien invasion. After all, the USSR wanted to expand in Europe. Our minds as well as our bodies were in danger. Hollywood reacted to the political and cultural unease. A venerable genre, the Western, became darker in mood—questioning, in films like John Ford's *The Searchers* (1956), the vision of the West as a promised land. Here John Wayne, the archetypical American hero, is portrayed as an obsessed, perhaps even unhinged remnant of the confederacy with an all but psychotic hatred of Native Americans. The Western hero became a troubled soul, much like the superhero in today's films. He bore the uncertainties of an age of anxiety (which was the name of a poem written by W. H. Auden in 1947). But the genre that most reflected the fears embedded in the cultural politics of the age was science fiction.

Science fiction film goes far back into film history. One of the most important silent films is *Metropolis*, made in Germany by Fritz Lang in 1927. Bizarre machines, a mad scientist, and a sexy robot figure in this film about class distinctions with the rich living in a futuristic city while workers toil in an underground hell. As old as it was, science fiction was not a very popular genre or considered—with few exceptions—a prestige genre, even in the 1950s when it underwent a renaissance. Usually low-budget productions, they made do with often crude special effects and a great deal of oppressive mise-en-scène. Sometimes they were truly horrific, like *The Thing from Another World* (Howard Hawks, Christian Nyby, 1951), where a giant humanoid vegetable invades an arctic outpost. Occasionally high-profile productions were made, like *The Day the Earth Stood Still* (1951), a Christian allegory with a suave space visitor named Klaatu who comes with a message to save the Earth lest it be destroyed by a giant robot named Gort. In *War of the Worlds* (Byron Haskin, 1953), Martians all but obliterate Earth. *Forbidden Planet* (Fred Wilcox, 1953) was made by MGM, a prestige studio, in color and with stunning special effects that influenced later films like *2001: A Space Odyssey* (Stanley Kubrick, 1968) and the first *Star Wars* (George Lucas, 1977). *Forbidden Planet* is a futuristic retelling of Shakespeare's *The Tempest* and features an excellent robot named Robby (Figure 9.1).

Among all the alien invasion films that popped up during the 1950s, one stands out as the most interesting and controversial of the lot. A low-budget film from a minor studio, Allied Artists, Don Siegel's *Invasion of the Body Snatchers* (1956) has been called both pro- and anti-McCarthy, a work that condones the suppression of "otherness" ("Communists" in this case) in the form of alien invaders that take us over, or anti-conformist, a film that warns against losing our individuality. Even the film's makers were not sure where it was headed and created a wraparound for the main narrative, with a raving Dr. Miles Bennell, the film's central character (played by Kevin McCarthy), held in police custody, telling his story to a psychiatrist.

Figure 9.1 Robby the Robot in *Forbidden Planet*.

And what a story it is. Falling from the sky are huge pods that burst open, extruding exact duplicates of people who, in their sleep, are taken over by their emotionless double. The resulting pod people are like the living dead, without the blood and lurching walk. They are emotionless, and their apparent goal is to place more pods in people's houses in order to create more pod people. Much of this, especially in the early part of the film, is done in a gray-toned, claustrophobic atmosphere of increasingly challenged normality.[3] In a small town (Santa Mira, California), Dr. Miles Bennell, and his girlfriend, Becky (Dana Wynter), hear increasing reports from relatives and patients about how their loved ones have changed. They look normal, they seem to behave normally, but something is wrong. The town psychiatrist, who has already become a pod person, blames the problem on "worry what's going on in the world, probably." The worry grows in the course of the film as Miles and Becky become more convinced of the real problem. What's going on in the world is that the world is being taken over.

There are startling scenes: Miles and Becky visit their friends Jack and Teddy. Jack has discovered his simulacrum being formed on the billiard table in his darkened rec room (Figure 9.2). A poster reading "Mirroir Noir," "Black Mirror," hangs on the wall, echoing what is happening to the people on Earth as they become emotionless reflections of themselves. As Jack dozes off, the creature on the table comes to look like him. They find bubbling pods in the greenhouse, foaming, bursting open with yet unformed pod people popping out. The more Miles and Becky learn about what is happening, the more frantic they

Figure 9.2 Miles Bennell (Kevin McCarthy) discovers the simulacrum of his friend in *Invasion of the Body Snatchers*.

Figure 9.3 Miles reacts to the discovery that his girlfriend Becky (Dana Wynter) has become a pod person.

become as everyone around them changes into pod people. Their hysteria grows. Eventually, the police and the townspeople come after Miles and Becky, the only two left uncloned. With the town's warning siren blaring gratingly on the soundtrack, they flee into the hills. They hear music—a sign of civilization—but no, it is coming from a farm, preparing alien pods for further takeovers. Miles and Becky run and run until, exhausted, Becky falls asleep and becomes a pod person (Figure 9.3).

In case anyone watching *Invasion of the Body Snatchers* is uncertain of its message, the town's psychiatrist, himself a pod person, explains to a skeptical Miles:

> Santa Mira was like any other town. People with nothing but problems. Then, out of the sky, came a solution. Seeds drifting through space for years took root in a farmer's field. From the seeds came pods, which had the power to reproduce themselves in the exact likeness of any form of life ... Suddenly, while you're asleep, they'll absorb your minds, your memories, and you're reborn into an untroubled world.

"Where everyone's the same?" asks Miles, wondering if he will still love Becky. "There's no need for love," answers the psychiatrist. "Love, desire, ambition, faith, without them life's so simple, believe me." A perfect totalitarian world.

This was the great American fear in the 1950s. Conformity, loss of freedom and individuality, being taken over by an alien ideology. Don Siegel, the film's director, insisted *Invasion of the Body Snatchers* was an anti-McCarthy film, a warning against mob action and conformity.

But the tenor of the film, its language and perspective, suggest the opposite—that it is a warning against the Red Menace. But the ambivalence is important, and it is what keeps the film alive. Miles and Becky are pursued by mobs of pod people and must take to the hills where Becky finally succumbs and becomes one of them. Are they the last individuals left? The last to fight against conformity? Or do the pod people represent Communists, intent on invading our lives? Miles, presumably the last man alive, is left standing in the middle of the highway, as a truck carrying pods rushes by. He cries out, in hysterical closeup, directly at the audience: "You fools . . . You're in danger . . . They're here already . . . You're next." But studio fears insisted on that wraparound in which Miles goes to the police, who, perhaps, have not become pod people and believe his story.

Science fiction audiences did not need reassurance or ambivalence, only reinforcement of their beliefs. *Invasion of the Body Snatchers* was not a commercial success in the mid-50s, perhaps because it hit too close to home or was too vague in its politics. But its resonance continues and critics have noticed that it addresses not only the "Communist threat" but also more subtle fears of racial otherness, of immigrant labor—something suggested by the discovery of the pod farm in the California hills—even fears of female predation signified by a suddenly monstrous Becky when she succumbs to the pod.[4] The fecundity of the film, despite or even because of its ambivalence, was sufficient for it to be remade at least three more times, with somewhat less of an ideological charge, but still imbued with the fear that we are permeable to alien takeover. It appeared in 1978 under its original title, directed by Philip Kaufman, then in 1993 as *Body Snatchers*, directed by Abel Ferrara, and in 2007 as a Daniel Craig/Nicole Kidman vehicle, *The Invasion*, directed by Oliver Hirschbiegel. A fourth version is being prepared. Zombie movies are themselves distant relations of the original. Even with the Cold War over, the notion of the alien other remains a powerful fear. Whether it's the uncanny belief that we have a malevolent double, or a larger cultural-political fear of a foreign ideology, the body remains a vulnerable site that the movies are always ready to exploit.

Notes

1 For a graphic visualization of deaths during WWII, see www.huffingtonpost.com/2015/06/06/world-war-two-fatalities-visualized_n_7526390.html.
2 See Frances Stonor-Saunders, *The Cultural Cold War: The CIA and the World of Arts and Letters* (New York and London: The New Press, 2015). A pictorial history of the Cold War is at www.history.com/topics/cold-war.

3 The claustrophobia of the film's mise-en-scène is pointed out by Barry Keith Grant, *Invasion of the Body Snatchers* (London: BFI and Palgrave Macmillan, 2010), 24.
4 See Katrina Mann, "'You're Next!': Postwar Hegemony Besieged in *Invasion of the Body Snatchers*," *Cinema Journal*, Vol. 44, No. 1, 2004, 49–68, and Grant, 77–92.

Further reading

Barry Keith Grant, *Invasion of the Body Snatchers* (London: BFI and Palgrave Macmillan, 2010).

Constance Penley, ed., *Close Encounters: Film, Feminism, and Science Fiction Film* (Minneapolis, MN: University of Minnesota Press, 1991).

David Seed, *American Science Fiction and the Cold War: Literature and Film* (Chicago, IL: Fitzroy Dearborn, 1999).

Vivian Sobchack, *Screening Space: The American Science Fiction Film*, 2nd ed. (New York: Ungar, 1987).

J. P. Telotte, *Science Fiction Film* (New York: Cambridge University Press, 2001).

10 The Cold War, part two
Point of Order (1964) and *Dr. Strangelove or: How I Learned to Stop Worrying and Love the Bomb* (1964)

In this chapter, I want us to look at two films that apparently could not be more different—one is a documentary, or more appropriately a compilation of found footage; the other a fiction film, a carefully crafted satire. But each addresses an aspect of the Cold War in very different ways than *Invasion of the Body Snatchers*. Rather than collude with the fears of the Cold War audience as *Invasion* does, they confront, reveal, and, in the case of *Dr. Strangelove*, mock them. *Point of Order* allows the evil of McCarthyism to expose itself by showing McCarthy at his most malevolent and undone by a simple question. *Strangelove* exposes the madness of the Cold War through exaggeration and dark humor, ending with the end of the world. Both, released in the same year, provide a healthy antidote to the toxic atmosphere of the 1950s.

Joseph McCarthy was dead by 1956. Like all tyrants, he reached too far; his crazed obsession with finding Communists, which he never succeeded in doing, led him to attack the army, accusing it of harboring Communists and holding hearings about its alleged wrongdoing. The particulars of the hearings are complex because they involve not only McCarthy's attack on the army, but the army's attack on McCarthy and his committee for requesting special treatment for G. David Schine, a friend of McCarthy's legal counsel, Roy Cohn. Those two had toured Europe and demanded that some 30,000 books be removed from the libraries of the United States Information Service. Their actions and recommendations reminded many of Nazi book burnings.[1] The corruption inherent in all of this could hardly have gone unnoticed, but McCarthy was willing to risk everything by investigating the army. The Army–McCarthy hearings were televised, allowing people a close look at this grinning, giggling, alcoholic sociopath. The American documentarist, Emile d'Antonio, put together found footage, television kinescopes—film made by a camera pointed at a television screen—of those hearings and edited them together into his 1964 film. McCarthy had, during his lifetime, already been exposed on television by newsman Edward R. Murrow in a courageous act of journalism. He had, then, already been weakened, and the results of the army hearings were deadly for him. After the hearings he was censured by the Senate; he had reached too high and in 1954 his power was revoked. Then he died.

Despite the ten-year lag, and made in the middle of the decade that witnessed a counter-cultural revolt against not only the Vietnam War, but the politics of the Cold War itself, de Antonio's film became a riveting reminder of just how mean-minded and absurd the anti-Communist witch hunts were. Except for the beginning, which situates the film in its time and place, *Point of Order* is without narration, using only subtitles to identify the various members of McCarthy's Permanent Subcommittee on Investigations, members of the army, and their attorneys. Other titles announce the various aspects of the investigation. Otherwise, the viewer is left alone with a torrent of words emerging from the murky, fuzzy, claustrophobic images of the committee room. It is riveting, uncomfortable viewing.

The film is edited for maximum suspense and a satisfying conclusion. De Antonio is free to construct his documentary to achieve the impact he wants while remaining true to the content of the images and the complexity of its politics. He intercuts reaction shots that may or may not have occurred in reaction to what we have just seen. But this does not falsify anything about the hearings themselves; it only structures and gives necessary form to the bits of kinescope that de Antonio had at his disposal. Through his editing, he captures the inherent drama of the proceedings and allows it to achieve a climax that may not have been the actual climax of the hearings themselves, but constitutes a signal of the end of McCarthy's career.

The army's chief attorney was a folksy, soft-spoken, elderly New England gentleman named Joseph Welsh. He challenged Roy Cohn to produce the number of Communists or "subversives" that McCarthy charged were at large in the defense industry. Cohn was an extraordinary piece of work, perhaps even more mean-minded than his boss. He prosecuted Ethel Rosenberg and was a mentor to Donald J. Trump. When Welsh confronted him with the exaggerated challenge to get those Communists identified by the end of the day, McCarthy uncoiled a full reptilian attack. He singled out Frederick Fisher, an associate of Welsh, and accused him of being a member of a Communist organization. But this time he attacked someone unwilling to be cowed or victimized, and Welsh was ready with a response. McCarthy tried to

The Cold War, part two 113

Figure 10.1 "At long last . . . have you left no sense of decency?": Joseph McCarthy, Roy Cohn, and Joseph Welsh in *Point of Order*.

interrupt by asking for the information on Fisher. Welsh assured him that it was true that Fisher once belonged to a left-wing group but was now a good Republican. He also had warned Fisher that McCarthy would attack and told him he would not put him on the committee. Welsh went on:

> Until this moment, Senator, I think I never really gauged your cruelty and your recklessness . . . Let's not assassinate this lad further, Senator . . . You've done enough. Have you no sense of decency, sir, at long last? Have you left no sense of decency?

There continues a back and forth (Figure 10.1), Welch refuses to discuss the matter further, and applause rings out from the audience. The film ends with McCarthy ranting about Communists as the hall empties out.

That question, "Have you left no sense of decency?", pretty much finished McCarthy's career. And it is amazing in retrospect that all it took was one person to say "no" to him, to call him out on his "cruelty and recklessness." Amazing too that we have such a powerful record of this in de Antonio's film. In recent years, the "media" have come under attack from the country's leadership, taking offense when "cruelty and recklessness," not to mention lies, are exposed. In response, populist, online media have emerged, some of which spread the very lies that it is the duty of the media to debunk. It is a difficult quandary, a nasty cycle of gamesmanship that hurts the culture and damages the body politic. But there still remain journalists and filmmakers who are willing to take the risks of exposing wrongdoing and downright political and cultural corruption. Sometimes it takes more than the authoritative voice of an individual, or an equally authoritative media, to call out dishonest, hurtful, even deranged behavior. Sometimes it takes just one person discovering old film in a scrapheap to remind us of "cruelty and recklessness."

In lieu of documentary footage, it may take the excoriating voice of pitiless satire to reveal bad behavior or at least make plain how stupid and damaging that behavior can be. Satire is a difficult genre to pull off. To give it authority, it takes an authoritative voice, direct or filtered through the narrative, to give it strength and conviction. It takes a formal elegance that might be brutal in its honesty, but rigorous in its structure, and it takes a strong focus on the absurdity of the individuals in the political drama being satirized. Satire must be rooted in political reality while turning that reality into an absurd but not unbelievable fiction. A target, the turning of real-life characters into exaggerated types of bad behavior, a strong moral voice: all of these conditions are met in Stanley Kubrick's great 1964 Cold War satire, *Dr. Strangelove or: How I Learned to Stop Worrying and Love the Bomb*.

So far, we have been talking about the politics and provocateurs of anti-Communism. But there was another major, more deadly, Cold War component: the reality of atomic warfare due to the buildup of nuclear arms by the implacable Cold War antagonists. The U.S. and the USSR played a deadly game that involved fighting over which one would have the greatest stockpile of nuclear weapons ready to fire at the other. The competition devolved into standoff, appropriately called MAD: Mutually Assured Destruction. The theory was that each side would be so frightened by the specter of total nuclear annihilation that they would never use their weapons. That theory was sorely tested by the Cuban missile crisis of 1962, when a horrifying nuclear standoff took place between the two world powers. Russia planted nuclear-tipped missiles in Cuba. President John F. Kennedy set up a naval blockade around Cuba and was ready to press the button. Russia backed down when the U.S. promised to remove missiles pointed at the USSR in Turkey and to refrain from invading Cuba (as it had done in the Bay of Pigs fiasco a year earlier). For thirteen days, the world was on the brink of nuclear destruction.[2]

Stanley Kubrick, with some assistance from author Terry Southern, was thinking about a serious film about the nuclear threat based on a novel called *Red Alert* by British author Peter George. The more they thought about it and the more they read about it, especially Herman Kahn's *On Thermonuclear War*, a serious book that proposed how the world might survive nuclear Armageddon, the more they realized that this was the stuff of dark humor. The notion that serious men were enabling the destruction of the world as part of ideological gamesmanship was impossible to be taken seriously. It was too serious, too frightening, too absurd. The film that resulted from their

The Cold War, part two 115

collaboration and bemused horror is a comedic satire about the end of the world, brought about by lunatics, acting under a straitjacket of events and technologies they created with the sole purpose of taking their own destruction out of their control. *Dr. Strangelove* is a comic film about the human race committing suicide.[3]

The film's premise and construction are deceptively simple. The USSR has set up the Doomsday Machine: a device created to cover the earth in a radioactive shroud if either side makes a nuclear strike; Mutually Assured Destruction. At Burpelson Airforce Base the psychotic General Jack D. Ripper (Sterling Hayden) (Figure 10.2) worries about the loss of his fluids during sexual intercourse. His fears extend to the depletion of fluids worldwide, so he orders his bombers to bomb Russia, which will set off the Doomsday Machine. Ripper confronts his British aide, Group Captain Mandrake (played by the master of comedic face and voice, Peter Sellers (Figure 10.3), who has two other roles in the film), and delivers his paranoid explanation. He smokes a huge cigar and his face looms out of the darkness: "I can no longer sit back and allow Communist infiltration, Communist indoctrination, Communist subversion, and the International Communist Conspiracy to sap and impurify all of our precious bodily fluids." At long last, the madness of anti-Communist discourse is exposed as the ravings of a lunatic.

Figure 10.2 The face of nuclear madness: General Ripper (Sterling Hayden) explains his concern over his precious bodily fluids in *Dr. Strangelove or: How I Learned to Stop Worrying and Love the Bomb.*

Figure 10.3 Peter Sellers as Group Capt. Lionel Mandrake, trying to reason with Ripper.

Dr. Strangelove is full of lunatics, most of them with names that have vulgar sexual connotations, because Kubrick sees an odd but not necessarily crazy connection between sexual dysfunction and its sublimation into belligerence. Also, as satiric figures, they are not realistic characters, but condensates of various real-life people. President Merkin Muffley (also played by Sellers; his name alludes to fake pubic hair) (Figure 10.4) is a version of Adlai Stevenson, a two-time democratic candidate for President, whose intelligence was too much to get him elected. Muffley, however, is less intelligent and more befuddled than his real-life counterpart. General Buck Turgidson (George C. Scott), based on any number of gung-ho military men (General Curtis LeMay—who was called "bombs away LeMay," and who, during the Vietnam War wanted to bomb that country into the Stone Age—comes to mind), speaks, or rather rants, about "the Russkies." Nuclear war might not be so bad, he thinks: "I'm not saying we wouldn't get our hair mussed. But I do say no more than ten to twenty million killed. Tops. Depending on the breaks." He clutches a binder with the words "World Targets in Megadeaths." He tangles with the Russian ambassador, de Sadeskey, forcing the President to yell at them as if they were children: "Gentlemen, you can't fight here. This is the War Room!"

The Cold War, part two 117

Figure 10.4 Peter Sellers as President Merkin Muffley, talking to the Russian Premier.

The War Room is a huge, dark space, crowned by a circle of fluorescent lights and, on the wall, a huge map of Russia showing American planes slowly breaching its borders. Lurking in the shadows is Dr. Strangelove (Sellers, again) (Figure 10.5), an amalgam of several figures: Henry Kissinger, who was just getting started in his career as international trouble-maker, and Werner von Braun, one of the Nazi scientists brought to the U.S. after WWII to jumpstart its missile program. But Strangelove transcends the real-life figures from whom he is constructed. He is the dark angel of death; crippled Nazism, confined to a wheelchair until nuclear annihilation is initiated.

The film's satire is not only of individuals, but of their language itself, the language of sex and death, the deterioration of meaning, the collusion of nihilism. As the bombs rain down, Major Kong, the pilot of the B52 that evades Russia's attempts to shoot down the American planes invading the country under an agreement between President Muffley and Russian Premier Kissoff, rides a hydrogen bomb like a gigantic erect penis into the earth. The men in the War Room huddle together, talking about the ratio of men to women in the mines where they will take refuge during nuclear winter. They argue with the Russian ambassador, and Turgidson, playing on the Cold War language

Figure 10.5 Fascism is reborn in the War Room: Peter Sellers as Dr. Strangelove.

of a "missile gap," calls out, "We must not allow a mine shaft gap"—at which point Strangelove arises from his wheelchair, snaps a Nazi salute, and calls out, "Mein Führer, I can walk." Hydrogen bombs explode the earth. It's as chilling an ending as any film I can think of. These nutty characters, scurrying around the dark womb of the War Room, end up destroying themselves and everyone else.

An extraordinary thing about this extraordinary film is the way Kubrick condenses the complicated issues and personalities of the Cold War into a relatively short time within just three major locations: the interior of the SAC bomber headed to bomb Russia, the War Room, and Ripper's office. Perhaps the film is saying that it wasn't that complicated after all, that the principles in the Cold War were acting as such mindless fools that their actions were doomed to failure. There was, of course, no Armageddon. Not yet, at least. The Cold War ended by folding under its own weight. McCarthy was discredited. The U.S. was able to outspend the USSR in military buildup (President Ronald Reagan, who lived in a cinematic dream state, wanted to build a Star Wars missile shield to protect the U.S.), and the USSR collapsed into anarchy, kleptocracy, and oligarchy. There was no Communist infiltration or Communist indoctrination in the U.S., but there was and is, as Kubrick prophesized in his film, the threat of Fascism, of a "strongman" emerging who promises to make the country great if we only follow his lead, who talks in bellicose terms of "fire and fury." Who may even be worried about our precious bodily fluids.

Dr. Strangelove certainly outraged Conservatives in the United States, but did it change minds about the deadly absurdity of the Cold War? Probably not. Radical views tend to confirm the thinking of those who already hold those views. What did change minds was the sheer inventiveness of Kubrick's film. Its incisive view of military and political insanity had never been so well expressed, so well that it has become, long after its immediate targets have disappeared, something of a prophetic work. The very name "Strangelove" has entered the vocabulary, and the antics of the War Room speak still to military madness and the irrationality of political gamesmanship. As long as political language gets corrupted into destructive clichés, *Dr. Strangelove: or How I Learned to Stop Worrying and Love the Bomb* will remain relevant, hilarious, and scary.

Notes

1 See www.history.com/this-day-in-history/roy-cohn-and-david-schine-return-to-u-s.
2 For a history of the Cuban missile crisis, see https://history.state.gov/milestones/1961–1968/cuban-missile-crisis.
3 For the genesis of *Dr. Strangelove*, see Mick Broderick, *Reconstructing Strangelove: Inside Stanley Kubrick's 'Nightmare Comedy'* (New York: Columbia University Press, 2017).

Further reading

Michael Broderick, *Reconstructing Strangelove: Inside Stanley Kubrick's 'Nightmare Comedy'* (New York: Columbia University Press, 2017).
Margot Henriksen, *Dr. Strangelove's America: Society and Culture in the Atomic Age* (Berkeley and Los Angeles, CA and London: University of California Press, 1997).
Peter Krämer, *Dr. Strangelove or: How I Learned to Stop Worrying and Love the Bomb* (London: BFI and Palgrave Macmillan, 2014).

11 Hollywood and the blacklist
Salt of the Earth (1954)

One of the ugliest manifestations of the Cold War, equal in its destructiveness to Joseph McCarthy and his Senate Committee, was the House Committee on Un-American Activities, HUAC for short. Established in 1938 to hunt down "subversives"—mainly Nazis—its power waxed and waned until it went out of business in 1975. During its period of greatest power in the late 1940s, it went out of its way to ruin people's lives. But the main thing about HUAC is that it should not have existed in the first place. Its original head, Martin Dies, and one of its first members, John Rankin, were white supremacist supporters of the Ku Klux Klan and anti-Semites. Hardly a leadership devoted to impartial judgment about "subversives." But even more importantly, the very notion of judging and prosecuting "un-American activities" is absurd. What are American activities against which to judge as "un-American"? The first amendment of the Constitution guarantees freedom of speech, even when that speech is abhorrent, as in the case of white supremacists. Treason might be considered "un-American," and there are harsh penalties for its commission. Treason is a political act—spying for the enemy, for example, or divulging state secrets—but even these are dependent on whom we have presumed is the enemy. Nazi spies working against the country's interests during WWII would be committing treason. The U.S. was at war with a noxious power. But consider the case of Edward Snowden, who exposed government spying operations and divulged state secrets. He fled to (of all places) Moscow to escape prosecution. Some consider him a hero. Others a traitor. Was he committing "un-American" acts?

Indeed, a person may be a traitor from one political point of view and a resistance hero from another. During the postwar period, many thought they saw such matters clearly. Communists were bad; what's more, they were dangerous as global antagonists and internal disrupters. HUAC would have had us believe that all this was an imminent national threat. They had a spotty record in their early days. Looking for Communists was a hard job when there weren't that many to find. McCarthy succeeded for a while not by finding Communists—he didn't—but by making things up. HUAC had success in the late 1940s with the Alger Hiss case. Hiss was a State Department employee accused by ex-Communist Whittaker Chambers of being a Communist spy. Richard Nixon, who would be President in another decade, worked on the prosecution. Incriminating evidence against Hiss was found in a pumpkin on Chambers' farm. Yes, a pumpkin. Hiss, who had denied the charges against him, was convicted of perjury and served five years in prison.

But HUAC wanted something juicier, more appealing to the public than a government bureaucrat and a pumpkin. Shortly after it was formed, the Committee came to Hollywood to expose Communists in the movie business. But Hollywood in 1938, though still in the grips of the Recession, was running smoothly, and the studio heads, many of them Roosevelt supporters, wanted no part of investigations. They had, a few years earlier, settled the problems of censorship by setting up the Production Code that policed what could and could not be shown on the screen. Movie attendance was good, and movies were as popular as ever. Alleged Communists in their ranks did not worry them. The war changed all that.

Not that Hollywood didn't do well during the war. They poured their resources into the war effort, making films (that had to pass through the Office of War Information) that boosted morale. Many stars, directors, and even some studio heads got wartime commissions in the military. But at the same time, the government began to clamp down on a major studio profit center: ownership of the theaters that showed their films and that therefore guaranteed distribution. Vertical integration, as it was called, was ruled a monopoly practice, and in 1948 the studios were made to divest their theater holdings—a major hit to their bottom line. During the war, studio employees were getting restive. There were strikes against Disney in the early 1940s, and then against Warner Bros. and Paramount. Studio head Jack Warner watched from the roof of his office building as police clashed with strikers. The illusion that the studios were a happy family under the control of the benevolent despot of a studio head was shattered. Loss of control led to loss of confidence.

In 1944, a group of Hollywood conservatives, including John Wayne, Walt Disney, Gary Cooper, and a number of other actors, directors, and producers, formed the Motion Picture Alliance for the Preservation of American Ideals. The group was formed, allegedly, to fight Communism rife among Hollywood screenwriters.[1] There were left-wing screenwriters as well as other figures in the film business. Some of them were or had been members of the Communist Party. But the nature of the studio system, in which no single hand, short of the studio head and his delegated producer, had complete control over a film's creation and production, did not permit any "Communist propaganda" to enter a film unmodified. Never mind. They held left-of-center views and they had responsibility in making movies. There was a complicating factor: during the war, Russia was a U.S. ally. In good patriotic fashion, the studios made a few films favorable to the USSR. Warner Bros. made *Mission to Moscow* (Michael Curtiz, 1943) that soft-pedaled Stalin's grim show trials. Samuel Goldwyn's company made *North Star* (Lewis Milestone, 1943) about Ukrainian resistance against the Nazis. MGM made *Song of Russia* (Gregory Ratoff, 1944) in which a visiting American symphony conductor stays to fight the Nazis alongside his Russian girlfriend. These films would come back to haunt them.

Larry Ceplair and Steven Englund write:

> Like a beacon in the darkening political night of postwar America, Hollywood attracted the moths of reaction again and again. Ostensibly the attackers cried out against "Communist subversion" in film making, but in truth their main target was the populist and liberal themes which, in HUAC's eyes, appeared all too frequently in the films made by the artists, intellectuals, and Jewish businessmen who dominated an industry which in turn dominated the public imagination.[2]

HUAC exploited the vulnerabilities of the studios and their own desire for publicity. If they could attack the movies for "subversive" content, they could strike at the very heart of the cultural imagination. If they could take down big stars and "intellectuals" like screenwriters, they could demonstrate their power to the country at large. Feeling under government threat, the studio heads caved when HUAC returned in the late 1940s and opened their doors and their files to HUAC's all-too-ready prosecutors.

The hearings were a brutal circus of accusations and denunciations. They were show trials, perhaps not as physically lethal as those that Stalin held in the USSR—no one was killed as a result of them—but many people lost their livelihood, if not their lives. "Naming names" was an important part of the process. The Committee had all the names of writers, directors, and actors who may have had left-of-center

Hollywood and the blacklist 123

views or membership in the Communist Party, but that wasn't what they wanted. Witnesses had to humiliate themselves by informing on friends and colleagues. If they did not, if they defied the Committee, they were accused of perjury and were blacklisted. Perhaps the most famous informer, a namer of names, was the director Elia Kazan. When he was finished informing, and his career saved, he directed a movie, written by another informer, Budd Schulberg, called *On the Waterfront* (1954). This was a film that, under the guise of attacking corrupt labor unions, approved of and encouraged informing.

There were some who refused to cooperate with the Committee, refused to inform, and demanded that HUAC obey their rights to free speech and free association. They were found in contempt, and ten of them—all former or current members of the Communist Party—went to prison: screenwriters Alvah Bessie, Ring Lardner, Jr., John Howard Lawson, Albert Maltz, Samuel Ornitz, Dalton Trumbo; producer Adrian Scott; and directors Lester Cole, Edward Dmytryk, and Herbert J. Biberman. By one of the great ironies of this tawdry business, Lardner and Cole served at the same prison as J. Parnell Thomas, a former head of HUAC, who was guilty of misappropriation of funds.

While they were the only Hollywood figures to serve time, many others were figuratively imprisoned by losing their income. The same year that HUAC came to town, 1947, the studio heads held a meeting in the Waldorf Astoria Hotel in New York. Confronting the pressures of the hearings, stewing in their own insecurities about how to respond to the anti-Communist hysteria coming their way, fearful of the fallout from the case of the Hollywood ten, they made a statement that would have awful consequences:

> Members of the Association of Motion Picture Producers deplore the action of the 10 Hollywood men who have been cited for contempt by the House of Representatives. We do not desire to prejudge their legal rights, but their actions have been a disservice to their employers and have impaired their usefulness to the industry.
>
> We will forthwith discharge or suspend without compensation those in our employ, and we will not re-employ any of the 10 until such time as he is acquitted or has purged himself of contempt and declares under oath that he is not a Communist . . .
>
> We will not knowingly employ a Communist or a member of any party or group which advocates the overthrow of the government of the United States by force or by any illegal or unconstitutional methods.

Dozens of talented men and women were blacklisted. Some left the country. The great director Joseph Losey went to Europe and, in England, restarted his career. Jules Dassin, who had brought some neorealist techniques to his 1948 film *Naked* City, fled as well. Bertolt Brecht, living in Los Angeles at the time, was called before the Committee, swore he was not a Communist, and immediately left to settle in East Germany. After his prison term, Dalton Trumbo (like many others) went to Mexico, where he wrote scripts either under an assumed name or the name of the person who fronted for him. He wrote the script for *Roman Holiday* (William Wyler, 1953), fronted by Ian McLellan Hunter, and it won an Academy Award. Under the name of Robert Rich, he won another Oscar for the screenplay of *The Brave One* (Irving Rapper, 1956). Two brave filmmakers, Otto Preminger and Kirk Douglas, allowed his name to appear on the screenplays he wrote on two films released in 1960: *Exodus* (Preminger) and *Spartacus* (Stanley Kubrick). This effectively ended the blacklist some thirteen years and many ruined careers after it started.

I said these were two brave filmmakers, but two out of dozens is not a great average. The blacklist was made possible by massive amounts of cowardice and fear, not to mention score settling. It was politics at its most raw and petty, driven by the overriding politics generated by the anti-Communist hysteria that gripped the country as well as the studios. To give one example: in 1948, there was a script making the rounds of RKO called *I Married a Communist*. Howard Hughes, at that time head of the studio, offered it to various directors. If they turned it down, Hughes decided that they must be Communists and therefore ready to be blacklisted. The film was eventually made by Robert Stevenson under the title *The Woman on Pier 13* and, like all the anti-Communist films made as a sop to the Committee, it was a flop. From the petty to the large-scale firings, to the innocent people attacked by HUAC, the anti-Communist purge of the 1950s had national repercussions.

Salt of the Earth (1953–4) was a film made by blacklisted filmmakers in spite of—in the face of—the blacklist. It was written by blacklisted Michael Wilson, who went on to anonymously write *The Bridge on the River Kwai* (1957) and *Lawrence of Arabia* (1962) and, under his own name, *Planet of the Apes* (1968). It was directed by one of the Hollywood Ten, Herbert J. Biberman, who went on to write and direct a film called *Slaves* in 1969, though his career never quite recovered from his blacklisting. Paul Jarrico produced the film. He wrote *Song of Russia*, one of the films that got Hollywood into trouble in the beginning, and went on to write and produce a number of minor films and television shows after the blacklist. Among the film's actors (who were mostly local nonprofessionals) was blacklisted Will Geer. The female lead, Mexican actress Rosaura Revueltas, was deported before the film was finished and not permitted to act in her native country. Everything was done to try and stop the production. The head of the powerful International Alliance of Theatrical Stage Employees, a union friendly to HUAC, tried to stop filming. Local townspeople in New Mexico, where the film was made, burned down the offices of the International Union of Mine, Mill and Smelter Workers, the Union that helped finance the film.[3]

But the film got made and, despite all efforts to the contrary, got a limited distribution. It became a kind of underground, independent, perhaps even cult film, known by people on the left, but unseen until relatively recently when it received a small revival. And what is this film that caused so much opprobrium in its time? A pro-union, pro-woman, pro-solidarity story about how to overcome oppression and poverty. Visually, it has touches of Eisenstein, of Depression-era documentaries like *The Plow that Broke the Plains* (Pare Lorentz, 1936), and Italian neorealism. All in all, given its sympathies to workers and minorities, it was a "Communist" film, at least as America would have defined it at the time.

Seen objectively, *Salt of the Earth* is an occasionally awkward mix of endearing amateur acting and tendentious dialogue that tends to make clear, with minimum subtlety, the struggles the characters endure. But subtlety is not its point. Its characters are poorly paid for their dangerous mining work. They are behind in installment payments to the company. Their bosses are heedless and patronizing, bordering on cruel. The miners' wives are tired of doing the home labor for the mine laborers. Everyone—except the owners and the police—are oppressed by the treatment they receive from above and below. But, as we saw in *Lucía*, in a revolutionary—or in this case politically progressive—film, the conditions of oppression must be a prelude to some liberating act. In the Cuban film, only the pre- and post-revolutionary conditions are seen. *Battleship Potemkin* dramatizes a pre-revolutionary event. In *Battle of Algiers*, the Revolution has only just begun. There was no revolutionary condition in the America of the 1950s and there is none now; only the possibility of local action, of struggle for change.

The struggle in *Salt of the Earth* is on a small scale, a local strike, but a large plea for social and gender justice. The miners are painfully aware that because they are majority Mexican, the bosses treat and pay them poorly. Their strike is all the more powerful because of their status and their need to be recognized for their labor and for the basics of physical protection for their dangerous work. Their wives join the strike for better sanitation and the means to modernize their lives (they are still chopping wood to keep their homes warm). All this comes to a head with a mining accident, a catalyzing event. When an injured miner is pulled to safety, his union brothers refuse to go back to work. They stand stock still as the bosses order them back into the mines and taunt them with racial insults. The miners shut down the machinery and stand firm. Biberman creates a montage of machines gone silent and men standing stock still as the women, on a hill above them and in solidarity, hold up a sign: "We want sanitation not discrimination." The seeds of solidarity are sown.

But there is internal turmoil. The men confront the owners and, within their families, their own wives, who demand the same recognition as the men. At the start of the strike, the men refuse the women's help until the women begin to infiltrate the picket lines, first as preparers of meals for the strikers and then as equals. As the bosses get tougher, the women become more active and their lives as activists begin to interact with their men in unaccustomed ways. Again there are obstacles, this time in the form of "scabs," strikebreakers hired by the bosses to break the picket line. Ramon, one of the main characters of the film, confronts a strikebreaker and is taken to a cop car and beaten. His pregnant wife, Esperanza, goes into labor; their mutual suffering is superimposed one against the other through a montage of physical pain. Public and private struggle are intermingled. As the strike wears on for months, deprivation and racism continue and build. The Mexican workers are told to "go back where they came from." A familiar refrain. But hopeful signs grow as well, especially when other unions join the strikers in solidarity. They send food and money to the striking mine workers. But despite this hopeful turn, the owners get an injunction to stop the strike. This creates an opportunity to turn things upside down. The miners and their wives meet, and through careful parliamentary maneuvering, over the objection of the male members, the men accept the offer of the women to take over the picket line. All except for Esperanza, whose husband—like Tomás in *Lucía*—remains adamant in his righteous patriarchal role to keep her at home.

The gender shift is as important. The women had started by militating for better sanitation—basic living conditions. Now they are militating for the Union, their husbands, and workers' rights. But the history of labor in the U.S. proves that workers' rights are not easily won. The owners and their enforcers show no deference to the women. The sheriff, working for the bosses, runs down a woman in the picket line and then disperses the rest with tear gas. But the women fight back—physically beating the deputies off (Figure 11.1).

Hollywood and the blacklist 127

Figure 11.1 Solidarity: after fighting off the police, the women resume their demonstration for equality in *Salt of the Earth*.

Despite her husband, Esperanza joins in, disarming a deputy by knocking his gun down with her shoe. The sheriff rounds up the women and locks them up.

"Once these people get out of hand..." These are the worried words of the District Attorney, as the women, packed in a cell near his office, are yelling, "We want the formula," for Esperanza's baby, who has been locked up with her mother (Figure 11.2). In a significant moment, Esperanza, from her cell, shared with the other women, passes the baby to her husband, Ramon, who has so far refused to play house husband. Like the transfer of the women to the picket line, taking the place of the men, so the transfer of the baby to Ramon signifies a shift in responsibility and the recognition that men can assume roles that they have not only been unfamiliar with, but have denigrated. As the men work at unfamiliar homemaking tasks, they come to understand what their wives have gone through without such basics as hot water. Some come to understand women's demands for equality in all aspects of life. Ramon does not, and when Esperanza is released the two have a confrontation that ends with Ramon about to strike his wife. "Once these people get out of hand..." The official's concern spreads not only to the striking miners, but even more broadly to the shift in power between men and women.

Figure 11.2 "We want the formula!": the jailed women demand food for Esperanza's baby.

"These changes come with pain," says Esperanza's friend. In a lovely sequence, Ramon is walking in the woods, hunting with his friends, as the words of his wife, telling him that they can't merely fight for their rights, but win them, echo in his ears. At home, the company evicts the women from their homes. "Eviction," the women cry in a montage of worried and angry faces. Ramon returns and the men and their wives pour in from other mining sites, returning the household goods back into the homes of the dispossessed as quickly as the sheriff's men take them out. Faced with overwhelming numbers, the sheriff and the mine owner step down, "for now."

Like all the revolutionary and progressive films we have discussed, *Salt of the Earth* ends with affirmation. Even Ramon finally comes to understand the dignity of equality and communal struggle. The film itself is a testament to the courage of the blacklisted individuals who made it. And there is no question but that unions made progress even in the oppressive 1950s. HUAC itself tried to press on with its dirty work. In 1960, they had a film made of their opprobrious hearings in San Francisco, where protestors were fire-hosed down the steps of City Hall where the hearings were held. They called it *Operation Abolition*, believing that the Communists were responsible for the protestors who wanted the Committee "abolished." Abolition did not happen for another nine years, but the documentary was seized on by the burgeoning counterculture and turned against the Committee, its brutality made physically apparent. The blacklist itself came to an end in the early 1960s, but its stain has never quite been rubbed out. When Elia Kazan was awarded an honorary Oscar in 1999, there were protests from surviving blacklistees as well as members of the film community who still would not countenance his behavior.

The stain of HUAC may eventually be erased as its victims and their memories die. But the fact is that societies seem to need an enemy and an internal "watchdog" group to fight them. Now in the 21st century there is a quest for "enemies," for groups to blame, for alien ideologies without which we might be safe. The reality is that there are always enemies and there are always cultures and beliefs that seem strange to us. None of this is an excuse for individual, cultural, or political paranoia. Luckily there are a variety of tools to combat this paranoia, including the fictions that we make to respond to it. Movies and, more recently, television and streaming services have created fictions that keep us aware of paranoia and political innocence and ignorance. Few are revolutionary; most are dark and troubling.

Notes

1 See http://encyclopedia.jrank.org/articles/pages/2921/The-Motion-Picture-Industry-During-World-War-II.html.
2 Larry Ceplair and Steven Englund, *The Inquisition in Hollywood: Politics in the Film Community, 1930–1960* (Berkeley and Los Angeles, CA: University of California Press, 1983), 254.
3 The production history of *Salt of the Earth* can be found in the entry for the film in the American Film Institute Catalogue, www.afi.com.

Further reading

Larry Ceplair and Steven Englund, *The Inquisition in Hollywood: Politics in the Film Community, 1930–1960* (Berkeley and Los Angeles, CA and London: University of California Press, 1983).
J. Hoberman, *An Army of Phantoms: American Movies and the Making of the Cold War* (New York: New Press, 2011).
Frank Krutnik, Steve Neale, Brian Neve, Peter Stanfield, eds., *'Un-American' Hollywood: Politics and Film in the Blacklist Era* (New Brunswick, NJ: Rutgers University Press, 2007).
Jon Lewis, "'We Do Not Ask You to Condone This': How the Blacklist Saved Hollywood," *Cinema Journal*, Vol. 39, 2000, 3–30.
Victor S. Navasky, *Naming Names*, 3rd ed. (New York: Hill and Wang, 2003).

12 Paranoia and political assassination
JFK (1991)

The Cold War was the era of paranoia, from the very real fears of nuclear war to the absurd fears of domestic "Communist subversion." But the fact is that politics in general is a paranoid game. One side creates fear of the other, or at least fear of their policies. Politics plays on more general fears, of the economy, of national security, of migrants, of people of different colors and genders. Paranoia travels around and across the political spectrum from left to right. Fear and suspicion, sometimes real, often unfounded, are politics' life blood. There is a famous book by the historian Richard Hofstadter called *The Paranoid Style in American Politics*. Published in 1954, as a response to the growing power of the right wing in the U.S., its insights are undiminished:

> The modern right wing ... feels dispossessed: America has been largely taken away from them and their kind, though they are determined to try to repossess it and to prevent the final destructive act of subversion. The old American virtues have already been eaten away by cosmopolitans and intellectuals; the old competitive capitalism has been gradually undermined by socialist and communist schemers; the old national security and independence have been destroyed by treasonous plots, having as their most powerful agents not merely outsiders and foreigners but major statesmen seated at the very centers of American power.[1]

Substitute "elites" for "major statesmen" and Muslims for "socialist and communist schemers," and you may hear echoes of recent political campaigns in the U.S. as well as the United Kingdom and Europe.

Paranoia can exhibit itself in a variety of ways, from smoldering resentment and anger over the belief the government isn't treating you well, to believing or even spreading conspiracy theories about hated

Paranoia and political assassination 131

politicians, to voting for candidates who seem to but really don't have one's interests in mind, to trolling people who hold a contradictory position (internet trolling and shaming is a cause of paranoia itself), to outright violence. Among the worst ways that violence can express itself is in the act of assassination. The desire to kill a politician may not necessarily emerge solely from paranoia. Some deeper political grievance might be the cause, as was the case of the murder of Archduke Ferdinand by a Serbian nationalist in 1914. The act grew out of anger and resentment at the annexation of Bosnia by the Austro-Hungarian Empire. The result of the assassination was WWI. From anger, hatred, and fear large catastrophic events in the political and global spheres can occur.

Paranoia in the United States also takes a variety of forms. As noted, the populist movement (which is by no means restricted to the U.S.) exhibits its fear and suspicions about people of color, immigrants, gender difference, "elites." It traffics in conspiracy theories and fake news. On the left and the right there is suspicion of government surveillance and corporate power. Rampant in politics and in the culture itself, paranoia manifests itself in the culture's imagination. In film, such cultural discomforts find a voice. We have seen how the Cold War threw off a number of films that addressed cultural anxieties about Communist infiltration in the form of stories about aliens invading from space. But there are also films that give paranoia a direct political voice. John Frankenheimer's 1962 film, *The Manchurian Candidate*, combined fears of Communist takeover with rumors of the brainwashing of American soldiers captured during the Korean War, along with a prophetic view of the assassination of political figures. *The Manchurian Candidate* is a hard-edged, slightly ironic (if not entirely self-aware) film that attacks McCarthyism while confirming that Communism is a threat. In parts sentimental, in its best parts surreal and dreamlike, the film snakes around the brainwashing of an American soldier who, directed by his Communist mother, plans the assassination of a political candidate. The cold brutality of the film is undercut by a romantic subplot, but it otherwise remains an interesting coda to liberal Cold War paranoia that insisted on the reality of "Communist indoctrination" while being against the crudeness of McCarthyism. *The Manchurian Candidate* is a fevered paranoid nightmare about cold-blooded political manipulation by any and all means.

After large political upheavals, paranoia can become a large-scale response that infuses the culture as a whole. After the revelations of illegal activity leading to the resignation of President Richard Nixon, there was wholesale suspicion of government and, given the amount of spying Nixon undertook against his enemies real and imagined, a cloud of paranoia which made itself known in a number of films. Alan J. Pakula's *All the President's Men* (1976), based on the newspaper reporting that helped bring Nixon down, is a combination of dogged journalism and paranoid threat in the search of the truth behind the Watergate break-in and the subsequent discovery of widespread corruption. Pakula was a talented director of paranoia, able, in this film, to generate a sense of looming threat to the reporters who unravel the complex entanglements of political wrongdoing.

In 1974, Pakula made a different paranoia film, this one about assassination. *The Parallax View* is a fiction about a mysterious corporation that assassinates political figures. The sense of threat in this film lies not only in the ultimate death of its central character (played by Warren Beatty) at the hands of the Parallax Corporation, but in the pervasive lack of explanation or rationale for the killings. As he would go on to do in *All the President's Men*, Pakula creates threatening spaces and, in this film, a mysterious indoctrination montage the corporation uses on its inductees. The film is bookended with the looming image of a Congressional review committee insisting that the assassinations it has been investigating are not the result of a conspiracy, but of a gunman acting alone. This would immediately remind a contemporary audience of what was a most potent source of mid- and late-20th-century paranoia, the assassination of President John F. Kennedy on November 22, 1962.

The assassination of Archduke Ferdinand precipitated a World War. The assassination of the 35th President caused a shudder through the culture and a sense of incredulity that such a monstrous act could have been carried out by someone acting alone. The shots fired at the President's motorcade from a high floor by Lee Harvey Oswald, the live-on-television murder of Oswald a few days later, the deaths of various other people connected, however tenuously, with the assassination, the subsequent Warren Commission report that held back crucial information—all created a pervasive sense of uneasy disbelief. Who killed Kennedy? Why was Kennedy killed? How could a single bullet cause the amount of damage it did? These questions swirl around the event even today, even as the myth of John F. Kennedy has been eroded by knowledge of his multiple affairs, his attraction to gangsters, his slow coming to awareness of civil rights issues, his dangerous brinksmanship with the Soviet Union. Still, he had been a young, vital President. He had a sense of humor. His sudden death was almost too much to acknowledge or bear.

A slew of conspiracy theories followed upon the assassination and the Warren Commission report, all of them disputing the proposition

Paranoia and political assassination   133

of a lone gunman. Oliver Stone's 1991 film *JFK* pulls these theories together and presents not so much a conspiracy theory of its own but a strong push for inquiry into the competing truths of the event. The film stimulates inquiry by being itself an inquiry, and not merely into the JFK assassination, but into the ways in which we interpret the political world in general and images of that world in particular. The film reflects the very confusion of paranoid conspiracy theories by presenting a profusion of images, multiple narratives, and a complex montage structure that demands close attention. Stone is influenced to a certain extent by the montage theories of Sergei Eisenstein, whose *Battleship Potemkin* we studied in Chapter 2. He plays with the clash of images in rapid succession, mixing color and black and white, widescreen and grainy 16mm filmstock, fiction and documentary, many voices, many ideas, many conflicts. Unlike Eisenstein, however, Stone is not delivering a strong revolutionary message, but rather a collision of images that cohere in alternative narratives that seek if not to explain, then to further the enigma of the assassination with at least a possibility of an explanation.[2]

The very beginning of the film is surprising in its unexpected ordinariness. We see black-and-white, small-screen footage of Dwight David Eisenhower, who was President of the United States from 1953–61. Before that, he was Commander of the Allied Forces that helped defeat Germany in WWII. In his farewell address as President, he delivered a warning that surprised many people: he articulated the danger to the Republic of what he termed "the military-industrial complex," a political and economic force that could weigh "on our liberty and democratic processes." Stone does not let the speech play out uninterrupted. Foreshadowing the methodology he will use throughout the film, he inserts various images, of military hardware, of missiles being launched, of families at home. It presages a restless style in which neither the filmmaker nor the viewer is allowed to rest. And this is just the opening sequence. It continues with a rapid summary of John Fitzgerald Kennedy's brief presidential career, including the Cuban missile crisis and the deepening engagement in Vietnam, about which we hear Kennedy saying that, without the support of the South Vietnam government, "I don't think the war can be won out there. It's their war. . . ." The images, in black and white and in color, flash by rapidly, some just a few seconds in length. As Kennedy delivers a speech, ending with the words, "we are all mortal," Stone moves abruptly into the film proper with a black-and-white image of a car speeding by and a woman being thrown out. In her hospital bed she screams incoherently about Kennedy being killed, as Stone continues his montage of images, coming very briefly to rest on the assassination itself on November 22, 1963, though he saves the horrifying images of Kennedy's head being blown apart, captured on film by the amateur filmmaker Abraham Zapruder, until the end of the movie.

We have spoken about the Classical Hollywood Style and its ability to ease the viewer into an illusion of a seamless ongoing narrative. Stone is intent on cracking that style by bombarding the viewer, demanding she follow his line of thought, which does not move in a straight, comforting line. Stone's aim is to cause discomfort, to not only disrupt the narrative flow, but to disrupt the easy historical narrative of the single shooter, Lee Harvey Oswald. Yet, this is not an entirely avant-garde movie. Despite the use of documentary footage, mixed in with staged images, there *is* a narrative, which is controlled by New Orleans District Attorney Jim Garrison (played by Kevin Costner), whose prosecution of a case against Clay Shaw, who he believes was at the heart of the assassination of the President, climaxes the labyrinthine search in the attempts to find its way through mix-ups and misdirections.

"We're through the looking glass," Garrison says at one point (Figure 12.1). He is discussing the case with his associates, one of whom gives a background on Oswald. As she talks, Stone intercuts images of the creation of a *Life* magazine cover. This was, in fact, an image of Oswald that appeared on the cover of *Life* on February 21, 1964, holding a rifle, and it was very controversial at the time because it didn't look right (Figure 12.2). The shadows were wrong; the stance impossible, Oswald's head appears pasted on. Although it has subsequently proven to be probably authentic, Stone believes it a fake and the montage during this sequence shows the parts of the photograph being assembled using pre-Photoshop techniques of cutting and pasting.[3] This sequence summarizes the technique of *JFK* as a whole: building up a case against the single shooter by cutting in pieces of information. *JFK* is indeed like the other side of a looking glass, and a distorted one at that. Characters and their actions peel off the central narrative of Garrison's investigators, reflections of leads, guesses, and surmises. Images and ideas move rapidly, and we must be alert to see and grasp them all. Perhaps the most controversial of the film's narratives is Garrison's discovery of a gay underground of possible conspirators. Stone takes some care to keep this from turning into homophobia. The characters are bizarre, but they are no stranger than the "straight" figures who crop up during the investigation. Clay Shaw (played by Tommy Lee Jones in the film), Garrison's main target, was a gay man; whether there was a gay underground that was somehow involved in the assassination is a question. Stone, at least, seems to think so.[4]

Paranoia and political assassination 135

Figure 12.1 "We're through the looking glass . . .": Jim Garrison (Kevin Costner), the light shining on his glasses as if to echo his comment, talks to his assistants in *JFK*.

Figure 12.2 An image of the possibly faked *Life* cover picture of Lee Harvey Oswald.

More and more figures appear as possible witnesses and participants in a plot to kill the President. Small narratives are refracted off the core in the search for answers. One of the most intricate examples of this occurs when Garrison goes to Washington (Stone purposively creates an allusion to *Mr. Smith Goes to Washington*, even having Garrison, like Jefferson Smith, reverently visit the Lincoln Memorial). He meets with "X," a former military man, chief of "black-ops," a made-up character that serves Stone as a conduit for complex stories of cover-ups and conspiracies involving the military, the CIA, Cuba, the Vietnam War, and the assassination itself. Stone handles their conversation dynamically; the stories "X" tells are visualized in high-contrast black-and-white images. His is a compelling story of government and military wrongdoing and cover-up, of revenge for Kennedy's desire to end the Cold War, to pull out of Vietnam, to end the useless battle against Cuba. Stone sees the two men, sitting on a bench by the Washington Monument, often from a long distance, exposed and vulnerable as an incredible tale of coincidence and conspiracy unfolds.

The meeting with "X" constitutes the middle of the film. The last half is taken up by the trial of Clay Shaw that Garrison holds to prove that Lee Harvey Oswald could not have acted alone. During the trial, Garrison shows the complete Zapruder film of the assassination, showing Kennedy's head exploding from the impact of the assassin's bullet. It's hard to watch and even harder to accept that one man with a rifle could have done so much damage. Garrison loses the case, despite his passion, despite his reference to Kennedy as the dying King. The sentimentality of Garrison's plea for justice almost overwhelms the coolness of the film's complex structure. But one can allow Stone's occasional melodramatic touches. The raw bombardment of images, ideas, and surmises that constitute *JFK* calls out for some resolution, even the deeply contested one that says that Lee Harvey Oswald acted alone.

I'd like to try an unusual comparison between Oliver Stone's film and the Italian director Michelangelo Antonioni's 1966 film, *Blow-Up*. Antonioni was a second-generation neorealist filmmaker, whose style evolved into an intricate play of image and story about contemporary life being held in a kind of emotional suspension, an almost neurasthenic state of numbness to reality. *Blow-Up* was his first film in English and takes place in London. It concerns a fashion photographer, unrooted, unengaged, impulsive, unnamed, who takes pictures in a park and discovers he's possibly photographed a murder. He discovers this by successive blowups of the images that seem to reveal more and more with less and less definition, until they appear like a modern abstract painting. (All this is before digital photography, when camera negatives were developed in chemicals and then printed onto photographic paper, also developed in chemicals.) Plot summary does not capture the mystery and ambiguities of Antonioni's film, which, like Stone's, is an inquiry into ways of seeing, of perception, of making sense of images and the stories we want them to tell.

On its face, *Blow-Up* is a non-political film. It doesn't seem to have anything to do with mass movements or political figures. But in the broader sense of the term, it very much deals with the politics of engagement, of discovery and commitment, of individual responsibility and the attempt to perceive the real—to have agency over one's surroundings, over history itself. This is what Stone is attempting to do in *JFK*. Both films deal with the politics of information, the power of a multitude of often contradictory facts that must be sorted out to find a kernel of something: some act, some individual from which a truth can be extracted and built. Politics too often means the power of evading truth, of causing information to be distorted and the recipient of that information to be confused. In response, there is a counter-politics that insists that information be formed into some discourse or image that conforms in some way to what actually exists. The truth. The photographer in *Blow-Up* could not, ultimately, prove there was a body. Garrison could not, ultimately, prove a conspiracy to kill the President. But in both cases the filmmaker was in control of the search. Antonioni believed that illusion and reality, truth and fiction, would always be blurred. Stone was certain that, with hard work, truth might be discovered out of a heap of images. The politics of skepticism vs. the politics of hope.

JFK is a film of the political righteousness of the imagination in the face of the haze of political evasion: "Who killed Kennedy?" It is a question that may never be adequately answered, which may be the ultimate point of Stone's visual interrogation. Motives can be mysterious and remain so. Which is perhaps why Stone, soon after *JFK*, made a film about a President whose motives remain a mystery to this very day: Richard Millhouse Nixon. Where *JFK* is a jigsaw puzzle of a movie, Stone's *Nixon* (1995) is grand opera about a small man with big ambitions and a streak of self-hatred, insecurity, and paranoia that led him to corruption and eventual resignation. Stone continues the cutting style he used in *JFK*, but in *Nixon* the torrent of images and the fractured time scheme is even more Eisensteinian. He has actions that are repeated from different perspectives. When Nixon, after losing his bid for governor of California, gives his infamous press conference, he utters the now unforgettable line to the gathered newsmen, "you won't have Nixon to kick around anymore." Stone shows Nixon (marvelously played by Anthony Hopkins) delivering the speech, and on the words "kick around anymore," cuts to black and white with the words repeated. The effect is to present a kind of schizophrenia, a man detached from his own consciousness, his own language.

As in *JFK*, by the end of *Nixon*, Stone grows a bit sentimental about his subject. But the political imagination he showed in the first film carries over to the second. Both films engage the political imagination to probe mysteries and create out of the montage of events and evasions another montage of complex clarity—clarity that itself comes with the demand of careful attention that may not have ultimate truth as its goal but rather paths that may lead to some truths. Most of our movies offer simplicity rather than complexity. The films discussed so far offer the latter. The films and television programs to come in our next chapters pursue political complexity via the means of documentary and the analysis of contemporary political reality.

Notes

1 Richard Hofstadter, *The Paranoid Style in American Politics, and Other Essays* (New York: Vintage Books, 2008), 23–24.
2 For *JFK* as an alternative narrative, see Robert Burgoyne, *Film Nation: Hollywood Looks at U.S. History* (Minneapolis, MN and London: University of Minneapolis Press, 1997), 88–103.
3 See www.usatoday.com/story/news/nation/2015/10/20/newser-lee-harvey-oswald/74264150.
4 For a rebuttal to Stone's theory, see www.huffingtonpost.com/entry/lgbt-history-month-the-gay-man-charged-in-the-assassination_us_58076defe4b00483d3b5cdc4.

Further reading

Robert Burgoyne, *Film Nation: Hollywood Looks at U.S. History* (Minneapolis, MN and London: University of Minneapolis Press, 1997).

Robert Kolker, *A Cinema of Loneliness*, 4th ed. (New York: Oxford University Press, 2011).

Robert Brent Toplin, *Oliver Stone's USA: Film, History, and Controversy* (Lawrence, KS: University Press of Kansas, 2000).

13 Contemporary American politics
Documentaries

We have already analyzed a major political documentary, Leni Riefenstahl's 1935 Nazi propaganda film, *Triumph of the Will*. We took notice of an even earlier political film, the little 1896 film of candidate William McKinley crossing the lawn in front of his house. In post-revolutionary Russia, Dziga Vertov was making and mixing newsreels, politics, and his own point of view, culminating in *The Man with the Moving Camera* (1929), a celebration of the "Kino Eye," the all-seeing, all-creating, probing eye of documenting cinema. The modern American political documentary can be seen in Robert Drew's *Primary* (1960), which, with minimum commentary, follows John F. Kennedy and Hubert Humphrey as they cross the country seeking the Democratic nomination for President. It was an important entry in what came to be called *cinéma vérité*, documentary filmmaking that allows events to play out in front of the camera with minimum interference by the filmmakers and minimum guidance for the viewer save what is seen and heard on the screen. And there is Emile d'Antonio *Point of Order*, a collation of found footage of the Army–McCarthy hearings. This may be the ultimate in *cinéma vérité*, something like a second-degree documentary, taking television footage, itself an all but passive recording of the hearings, and editing it into a commentary-free exposé of rancid political theater. *Cinéma vérité* was never quite what it pretended to be because of the simple fact of editing. The most non-obtrusive footage (it can be argued that no footage is non-obtrusive, since the very presence of a camera changes the way people behave) still has to be put together to form a narrative. And a narrative, by definition, tells a story, and any story has a point of view.

Today, documentaries, especially political documentaries, rarely pretend to be neutral observations. A noteworthy practitioner of personal, political documentary filmmaking is Michael Moore, whose films essentially document his own thinking about what is happening in the political world. *Fahrenheit 9/11* (2004), a film that was enormously popular and influential, is, in some ways, like *Point of Order* in that Moore uses clips of television news to tell the story of George W. Bush's appointment to office by the Supreme Court in the 2000 election and our entry into the Iraq War. This found footage provides the points of reference for the swirl of events following 9/11. "Was it all just a dream?" are the first words uttered by Moore in voiceover. That controlling, ironic, gentle, and insistent voice marks the difference between Moore's work and de Antonio's, whose actual voice is never heard after a brief introduction to the film, attesting to its veracity. In addition to the found footage, there are in *Fahrenheit 9/11* direct interventions by Moore himself: interviews and attempted interviews in which the filmmaker pushes himself into the action.

In the end, the facts are not a dream and the results of the election are all too real. The political history is all too strange. At first it appeared that Al Gore won the presidency in the 2000 election, but after the Supreme Court stopped a recount in Florida, George W. Bush became the 43rd President of the United States. In the opinion of some, Moore included, the election was determined by the Court, not the voters, and therefore did not quite have the validity of a national referendum. Bush vacationed through his first months in office. And then came 9/11, followed by the Iraq War, a grinding war, based on the lie that Iraq had "weapons of mass destruction." Iraq was a needless war that resulted in thousands of deaths, the destruction of a country, and the rise of the militant group ISIS. Moore follows this history. He represents the destruction of the World Trade Center Towers by a black screen with noises on the sound track, followed by startled and frightened onlookers. He shows the infamous television footage of a paralyzed Bush, sitting in front of an elementary school classroom, not knowing what to do after getting word of the attack. He proceeds as a calm but dogged investigator into the odd facts following the attacks. For example, while all commercial flights were grounded after the towers fell, the government allowed many Saudi citizens, including relatives of the 9/11 mastermind, Osama Bin Laden, to fly out of the country. They had business relationships with the Bush family. Such revelations pour out, through interviews and found footage, some so bizarre that we can barely make sense of them. Moore drums in the contradictions of wartime lies, intercutting battle footage with interviews of the troops and statements by government leaders; he presses home the ironies of Bush and his supporters pressing the untruths of weapons of mass destruction, of Bush's declaration of "mission accomplished" while Iraq devolves into civil war.

Contemporary politics: documentaries 141

Figure 13.1 Guerilla filmmaking: Michael Moore attempts to waylay a Congressman to see if he would sign up his own son to fight in Iraq (*Fahrenheit 9/11*).

Fahrenheit 9/11 is a web of revelations, a sly film that, in the cliché of the time, "connects the dots" and reveals the painful realities of the Bush era, its foreign entanglements, its mishandling of intelligence, its going to war against the wrong country, its absurdities (a mother who was stopped by the TSA at an airport because she had a bottle of breast milk for her baby). And always the presence of Moore. Unlike documentaries in which the director remains removed and observant, Moore is unafraid to insert himself directly into his film or splice in footage of the old TV detective show *Dragnet*. He walks around the Capitol, buttonholing Congressmen to find out if they are sending their children to fight the war in Iraq (Figure 13.1). Most of them flee in embarrassment. But Moore is unembarrassed. He is angry and allows that anger to inform his movie.

Did the film embarrass the government? Did *Dr. Strangelove*, a fiction film, change any minds about the Cold War? *Fahrenheit 9/11* was enormously popular for a documentary, though it is difficult to tell whether it changed any minds—those in power or not. The war raged, and Iraq fell apart, leaving space for ISIS to form. In the wake of *Fahrenheit 9/11* there were a number of documentaries about the wars in the Middle East. Some, like Tim Hetherington's and Sebastian Junger's *Restrepo* (2010), focused on a troop dug in in Afghanistan. Others documented the torturing of prisoners during the battle itself: Alex Gibney's *Taxi to the Dark Side* (2007), and Errol

142 Contemporary politics: documentaries

Morris's *Standard Operating Procedure* (2008) about the prison at Abu Ghraib. Much was shown. Little was learned.

Past wars were sometimes brought up in documentaries as cautionary tales. Errol Morris's *The Fog of War: Eleven Lessons from the Life of Robert S. McNamara* (2003) focuses on the Secretary of Defense during the Kennedy and Johnson administrations. Perhaps "defocus" would be the more appropriate term for what Morris does. He allows McNamara, eighty-five when the film was made, with his slicked-back hair and disengaged manner, to talk—talk, talk, and talk at the camera. The composition of the frame is off balance—as off balance as its subject. Morris intercuts other voices, other images, but mostly *The Fog of War* turns into a gut-churning, almost unconscious confessional (for the audience if not the film's subject) about the mistake that was the Vietnam War, made by the man who was largely responsible for executing it (Figure 13.2). At one point, literally representing the "domino theory" that was foisted at the time—that if Vietnam fell, other South Asian countries would fall as well—Errol has rows of dominos placed over a map of the region. McNamara talks about the lies that Lyndon Johnson told that got the U.S. into the Vietnam War, while claiming that's irrelevant to the point he's making. "We were wrong," McNamara says, "but we had in our minds a mindset that led to that action. And it carried such heavy cost." The dominos fall. The public McNamara goes figuratively out of focus while a somewhat contrite McNamara, near the end of his life and too many dead soldiers and civilians later, comes to the fore. This is the politics of

Figure 13.2 Robert McNamara talks to President Lyndon Johnson in this clip from Errol Morris's *Fog of War*.

bad faith and bad conscience, though never explicitly stated as such by McNamara. A confession of having been wrong isn't enough to wipe out all that the Vietnam War meant and the deep cultural and political wounds it caused.

In the film's epilogue, over images of McNamara driving through Washington, Errol Morris asks offscreen why McNamara never spoke out against the war after he left office. "These are the kinds of questions that get me in trouble," McNamara responds. "You don't know what I know about how inflammatory my words can appear. A lot of people misunderstand the war, misunderstand me. A lot of people think I'm a sonofabitch." Morris asks if McNamara feels any responsibility for the war. Does he feel guilty? He refuses to answer, saying there are too many complexities for a simple answer. "Do you feel that you're damned if you do and damned if you don't, no matter what you say?" Morris asks. "Yeah, that's right. And I'm regrettably damned if I don't." Don't what? Claim responsibility for the war? He has already claimed that responsibility over the course of the film.

War, as we have seen throughout our study, is attracted to cinema and cinema to it. War is action, danger, heroism, explosions, all elements that the movies and many moviegoers gravitate toward. Critical films about war—fiction or non-fiction—are less popular. There were fiction films about the Iraq War, but with the exception of Kathryn Bigelow's *The Hurt Locker* (2008), about an adrenalin-fueled soldier whose job was to disarm improvised explosive devices, these did not do very well. In the end, the war was wished into invisibility and President Bush sank in popularity. We tend not to want to see our failures. The same is true about race. Despite the recent upsurge in films addressing the lives of African Americans, made in response to the outcry about the lack of such films, race remains America's deep wound. It will not heal; we tend to want to ignore its pain, but filmmakers insist on exposing it.

We began our study of political films with D. W. Griffith's *The Birth of a Nation*, whose racial politics were crude and abhorrent. I ended that chapter on an optimistic note, suggesting that we have come a long way since Griffith's racism. A long way in film, at least, from the stereotyped cringing and cringe-inducing antics of Stepin Fetchit, or the "Mammies" played by Hattie McDaniel, both African-American players from the 1930s through the 1950s. Stepin Fetchit's character is the stereotype of the shiftless, cowering underling, while the Mammy is the stereotype of the strong, bossy family retainer whose selflessness and wisdom keep things together. While it was a blessing to these and a few other African-American actors to have movie roles, those roles were the opposite of a blessing because they projected the worst attitudes toward people of color held by too many people who watched them on the screen.

The Civil Rights movement pushed American film into an embrace of more diverse characters of color, but still stereotypes were hard to avoid. There were the "Blaxploitation" films of the late 1960s and early 1970s, featuring strong black lawmen, like *Shaft* (Gordon Parks, 1971), or outlaws, as in *Sweet Sweetback's Baadasssss Song* (Melvin Van Peebles, 1971). These films, directed by African Americans, still traded in characters with exaggerated traits, as if it were necessary to move from subordinate to super-dominant roles, skipping over daily lives. Settling into films about ordinary lives came slowly and sporadically. Directors Spike Lee and Tyler Perry came at this from opposite directions. Lee has largely focused on extraordinary lives, as in his biography of Malcom X (1992); ordinary lives living through trying times, as in *Do the Right Thing* (1989); or the trying experiences of ordinary people in *Da Sweet Blood of Jesus* (2014). Perry focuses on the righteous and comedic aspects of middle-class life. He plays a parody of the "Mammy" in his gun-toting character Medea and is the poet of redemption through faith and common sense. His films can be sentimental and funny simultaneously, and he has been accused of trading in stereotypes. But there is both a quiet and raucous dignity to his films that mark them off from the general run of movies about African Americans.

But are these political films? Spike Lee's work certainly fits the large definition. He is concerned with questions of race in the culture; how people of color interact with each other and the larger white community. He maps tensions and antagonisms, power and agency, weakness and suffering. Perry's films seem to fit the old genre of domestic melodrama or comedy. They are political in an even broader, but no less important sense in their representation of the domestic order that, while comically disruptive, does and can exist among people of color. Their struggles can be dealt with through faith and common, or sometimes uncommon, sense. Tyler Perry has managed to work outside the Hollywood system, which, despite some small changes, is still not welcoming to minorities and women in the roles of producer or director. He has his own studio in Atlanta and works quite independently.

The past few years have brought a lot of attention to Hollywood's racial and gender problems, and there have been some gains. We spoke about the contemporary *The Birth of a Nation* in the first chapter. There was Steve McQueen's torture-filled *12 Years a Slave* (2013), and Ava DuVernay's *Selma* (2014), as well as her extraordinary Netflix documentary about race and the prison system, *13th*. There have been many smaller films about black life like the *Barbershop* series, each directed by African-American filmmakers (Tim Story, Kevin Rodney Sullivan, Malcolm D. Lee). Television has come around with shows like *Empire*, *Black-ish*, and HBO's *Insecure*. But representation does not guarantee comprehension or acceptance. No amount of films or television shows will heal the wound. The main hope is to keep talking about it, revealing it, politicizing it, plumbing its depths.

One documentary has done all of these in remarkable ways. *O. J.: Made in America* (not to be confused with the fictional series, *The People v. O. J. Simpson: American Crime Story*) is, superficially, in the tradition of contemporary documentary films: many talking heads, from people who knew O. J. Simpson to ordinary bystanders to his career and crimes, to the various characters that were part of his trial for the murder of his ex-wife and her boyfriend, to experts and authors. Their comments are interleaved with some original, but mostly found television footage, including the extensive television coverage of the trial.

The extraordinary power of this nearly seven-and-a-half-hour film, broken into five episodes, made for the Disney-owned sports network ESPN, is drawn not only from what the various participants say, but how their comments and the visual material that accompanies them are edited to create a complex argument. The film begins with an old, bloated Simpson giving testimony of prior arrests and then works backward to his childhood, his extraordinary early football career to his final incarceration. These elements are not presented chronologically. The first episode, for example, concentrates on his celebrity, but subtly branches to encompass Simpson's place in Los Angeles sports and celebrity culture, and most importantly, racial culture. It digs back not only into Simpson's past, but into the Civil Rights movement and the early hopes that African Americans would find some peace in California, only to discover that racism was as extreme there as in the South. Early in the series, Edelman focuses on the corruption of the LA police, whose near vendetta and unrelenting brutality against people of color set the stage not only for the Watts uprising of 1965, but for the events of Simpson's capture and trial, when African Americans refused to believe the police and took Simpson's side, believing, against all odds, in his innocence as a means of justifying the treatment they had experienced from the police.

But against this identification is a contradiction. Among the knotty problems the film investigates are the ways in which Simpson became integrated into white society. It tells about a group of black athletes who organized in the late 1960s to fight racism. Simpson refused to join. "I'm not black; I'm O. J.," he is reported to have said, wanting to prove himself based on his athletic ability rather than his racial identity or political beliefs. He didn't have "typical" black looks, an interviewee says. He did have the temperament of a transracial celebrity. But, the film insists, events and politics kept interfering in this desired transcendence of race. Martin Luther King is assassinated in 1968. Black athletes raise their fists in protest at the Olympics. Simpson attempts to stay outside the fray, parlaying his fame as an athlete to become a spokesman for rental cars (Edelman interviews the CEO of Hertz rental cars, who, taking a risk, hired Simpson for their advertising), for soft drinks. He became a movie actor, "a counter-revolutionary advocate"—someone, an old friend says, "who doesn't know who he is anymore." He wanted to erase race as a component of his life. He wanted, perhaps, to erase his life and function only as someone well known and admired.

O. J.: Made in America continues, throughout its length, to counterpoint the individual and the cultures with which he is in constant contention. Simpson successfully becomes part of the white world of celebrity. But, despite his turning against—or, more accurately, moving away from—his racial roots, the black community embraces him. The LA police continue their abuse: there was the vicious beating of Rodney King by the LAPD, caught on video in 1991, and the subsequent acquittal of the assailants. There was the killing of a black woman by a Korean grocery store owner, caught on video. The shooter was not sent to jail. An uprising of the African-American community set LA on fire. In the midst of these events, Simpson was found guilty of vicious wife abuse and sentenced to community service, time he served by golfing. The film builds a powerful case against Simpson as a controlling, jealous, violent man, still beloved by the people who knew and admired him.

When the climactic event happened, when Simpson was accused and tried of killing his ex-wife and her friend, the African-American community were unwilling to assume Simpson's guilt. Edelman presents in detail the events leading up to and including the famous 1995 trial. There is the Bronco chase through the LA freeways, broadcast on national television, turning it into "Los Angeles's largest party." Crowds, white and black, gather to cheer Simpson on and call out "Free O. J." In retrospect, this footage, intercut with interviews, indicates how the eventual trial will turn out. O. J. the celebrity trumps Simpson the murderer.

The TV footage of the actual trial is intercut with interviews and with the actions leading up to it. All the famous or infamous players are represented: Johnnie Cochran, Robert Shapiro, Christopher Darden, Marcia Clark, Judge Ito, Kato Kaelin; even a Kardashian turns up as a friend for the defense. The jurors Edelman talks to simply don't accept

Contemporary politics: documentaries 147

the facts of the case. This is the crux, not only of the O. J. Simpson trial, but of the documentary as a whole. A trial with all the facts ready in evidence against the defendant went bad. Incompetence on the part of the prosecution, cleverness on the part of the defense. Mark Fuhrman, the cop already discredited because of his history of racism, finds the missing glove in the back of Simpson's house. An incriminating piece of evidence. Shrunken from being soaked in blood, Simpson's hand swollen, the glove doesn't fit his hand. This leads to Johnnie Cochran's rhyme that sealed the case for the jury: "If it doesn't fit, you must acquit" (Figure 13.3).

Edelman weaves a complex, subtle tapestry of racial conflict and misunderstanding—or perhaps an understanding that is all too clear. The reactions to Simpson's guilt or innocence fell neatly across racial lines. Many African Americans thought him innocent, many whites guilty. The history of racial animosity in Los Angeles especially, but country-wide as well, created the divide. Simpson was eventually convicted in a civil trial brought by the victim's parents, and the monetary penalty helped to precipitate his decline. Edelman traces this pathetic fall from grace and into illegal activities that eventually put Simpson in jail (he has subsequently been paroled). But the film offers no easy answers, only troubling revelations about how race and racial attitudes distort the thinking and the actions of individuals and the culture as a whole.

What is unique about Edelman's documentary, what separates it from the small number of films about the African-American experience, is its very complexity. It offers no comfort or uplift, only discomfiting

Figure 13.3 "If it doesn't fit, you must acquit": at his trial, O. J. Simpson shows off the ill-fitting gloves found at the murder scene (*O. J.: Made in America*).

insights and troubling questions. The film is at the nexus of politics, culture, and ideology: political in its discussion of power relationships between the races, between the police and people of color and the judicial system's unsteady attempt to deal a fair hand. The culture as a whole—the film implies—is responsible for the ongoing tension between the races, for being unable to completely understand America's original sin of slavery, to admit it, come to terms with it, but never move on—as it should never quite do. The ideology of race is deeply ingrained and deeply contradictory. Only the relatively few members of the neo-Nazi right would openly admit to being racist (but even a few are enough). The rest of us believe we are not; some of us know on some level we are; all of us struggle to come to terms with the complex realities of race and our attitudes toward it.

Political films, whether about race, revolution, Fascism, right or left-wing ideologies, or the election of public officials, try to come to terms with the complexities of how we conduct ourselves privately and communally; they understand that the private and the public are barely separable. They dramatize or document, imagine or report on the power struggles of our lives, our communities, our history. At their best, they clarify the complexity of the political without diminishing that complexity. Their power is gained by means of the formal ingenuity their makers use to communicate the horrors of Fascism and racism and the brief exhilaration of revolution. Even when a film provokes racism, as is the case of *The Birth of a Nation*, it can serve as a lesson, a warning. Politics in any of its many forms cannot be ignored or denied, because it is about power and control, about life lived in the community of others.

Further reading

Donald Bogle, *Toms, Coons, Mulattoes, Mammies, and Bucks: An Interpretive History of Blacks in American Films* (London, New Delhi, New York, and Sydney: Bloomsbury Academic, 2015).

Ed Guerrero, *Framing Blackness* (Philadelphia, PA: Temple University Press, 1993).

Bill Nichols, *Representing Reality: Issues and Concepts in Documentary* (Bloomington, IN: Indiana University Press, 1991).

——— *Introduction to Documentary* (Bloomington, IN: Indiana University Press, 2001).

Monica White Ndounou, *Shaping the Future of African American Film: Color-Coded Economics and the Story Behind the Numbers* (New Brunswick, NJ: Rutgers University Press, 2014).

14 Contemporary American politics
New channels

With the exception of *O. J.: Made in America*, we have been analyzing unconventional fiction films exhibited in conventional ways: projected in movie theaters. You have most likely seen them on disc and a TV monitor, but originally they were meant to be seen on the big screen. In our concluding chapter, rather than concentrating on one or two films, I want us to consider fiction films and series made for network, cable, and streaming venues where some of the most interesting and adventurous political works are being produced and exhibited. A variety of politically themed TV, cable, and streaming programs have appeared in the past years: *Veep*, *Madam Secretary*, *The Americans*, *House of Cards*, to name a few, and full-length movies, many on HBO: *Game Change* (on John McCain's 2008 presidential campaign) and *All the Way* (on President Lyndon Johnson and the Civil Rights Act). These shows and movies focus on politics in the most familiar sense—on elected or appointed officials trying to make their way through an often corrupt political system, on the politics of spycraft during the Cold War in the case of *The Americans*, and on the politics of corruption in *House of Cards*.

In this chapter, I want us to consider political fiction on three television series that are broadcast on three different platforms: *Veep* on HBO; *House of Cards* on Netflix; and *Madam Secretary* on CBS. Then we will look at two HBO feature-length films: *Game Change* and *All the Way*.

Two popular political series look at politics either as a ludicrous joke or as a dark complex of profoundly corrupt intrigues. HBO's *Veep* has gone through seven seasons. Ostensibly about the first woman President (she serves for one year), Selina Meyer (played with a straight face by Julia Louis-Dreyfus) is part of a bumbling, foul-mouthed coterie of hangers-on, would-be power brokers, and failed elected officials. The show's vision of politics is of a profane joke; its cynicism is boundless. No one and no action is for the public good, including none of the characters, with the possible exception of Tony Hale's Gary, Selina's obsequious, always present "body man" (Figure 14.1). If Frank Capra's *Mr. Smith Goes to Washington* were turned on its head and its own cynicism washed of all sentimentality, then you would get an idea of what *Veep* and its creators have in mind. *Mr. Smith* insisted, against all odds, that innocence and righteousness would win out over corruption. *Veep* insists in its profane comic breathlessness that there is simply no alternative to the disengaged self-serving of its characters. And as funny as it is, as much as it doesn't take itself seriously, it is still relentlessly dark and pessimistic, if only by suggestion. The fawning, preening, narcissistic characters who scuttle across the series represent the exaggerated worst of what we think of our politicians. There is no notion of public service here or selfless obligation, only the opposite of both. *Veep* is more than political satire: it is political travesty and a hilarious antidote to the pious hypocrisies of actual elected officials.

House of Cards is of a different order of fictional political filmmaking. Where *Veep* is consistently silly, *House of Cards* is ironic and serious. Based on a British series about an unscrupulous Prime Minister and his scheming wife, *House of Cards* presents a politician whose quest for power is evil and murderous. Francis (Frank) Underwood (the initials on his cufflinks are "FU") and his wife, Claire (Robin Wright), do not hesitate to maim or kill those they cannot maneuver to their side. The couple will fix an election, drive a sitting President out of office so Francis can take his place, threaten war so

Figure 14.1 Selina Meyer (Julia Louis-Dreyfus) and her "body man," Gary (Tony Hale), in *Veep*.

that he can keep his position—and so on through seemingly endless permutations of wrongdoing, malfeasance, and malevolence.

Malevolence? There is a formal device that keeps Frank Underwood from being a completely off-putting character. From time to time, he speaks directly to the camera, taking the viewer into his confidence, slyly revealing his plans, communicating his great pleasure in doing dirty deeds. As played by Kevin Spacey, with a slight southern drawl, Francis is an intriguingly attractive scoundrel. His machinations and evil deeds are done with a knowing demeanor—he knows he's a fictional character whose actions are impossible, implausible, and therefore unthreatening and, dare I say, enjoyable. No one in "real life" could get away with such corruption, could put the nation in danger to maintain power, could view the world only in terms of his own satisfaction. Too far from real life? Here is Frank in an episode from 2017 (Figure 14.2). He addresses the camera as he is being inaugurated for the job he connived, cheated, and murdered for:

> And now here I am, President of these United States. You made this bet, America, you voted for me. Are you confused? Are you afraid because what you thought you wanted is now here? And there you are, staring back, slack-jawed, bewildered, wondering if this is what you actually asked for! This democracy—your democracy—elected me! And if you think it was hard getting here you are beginning to understand what I'm willing to do to stay. I look across this crowd gathered today, and I know that these are not my supporters. I'm looking at people who are waiting with a smile on their face for their turn, and the most vicious among them are the ones who are smiling and clapping the hardest. "Power is a lot like real estate"—remember?[1]

Yes, we remember well a President who mixed power, the presidency, and real estate, and we may consider that *House of Cards* is something like a parallel political universe in which the President is permitted to do exactly what he likes because he was put in office by some who are "the most vicious among them." We may not, in the U.S., have a head of government as amoral and malicious as Francis Underwood; but it is always amusing to see a political drama that brushes tantalizingly close to political reality.[2]

Madam Secretary is in many ways the most conventional political show of the three we're discussing (Figure 14.3). Appearing once a week for some twenty-two weeks a season (as opposed to some ten episodes per season of *Veep* and twelve for *House of Cards*, all of whose

Figure 14.2 Francis Underwood (Kevin Spacey) addresses us during his inauguration.

episodes are available at once, making it a potentially ten-hour movie; previous seasons of *Madam Secretary* stream on Netflix as well). As a network program, *Madam Secretary* is under the obligation to follow more conventional narrative and dialogue practices. There is no profanity (compare this with *Veep*, where the absence of profanity is the exception) and equal emphasis is put on politics and family. Elizabeth McCord (played by Téa Leoni) tries to balance her high-pressured work in an administration—whose political affiliation is unnamed—with her family life. And, although some thematic elements flow through a season, the main problems set up in an episode are solved within that episode. In short, the Secretary of State solves a major world crisis and a minor family one through the force of her personality in less than forty-five minutes. The compactness of plotting, the precision editing, and the committed performance of the ensemble cast make the absurdity of a rapid resolution of overwhelming geopolitical crises seem plausible. It is a convincing and welcoming fantasy.

Behind these resolutions of global problems is a deeply moral sense of doing the right thing for the appropriate causes, which gives *Madam Secretary* a liberal tilt. The first episode of the 2016 series, directed by actor Morgan Freeman (who is also one of the show's producers) and written by Barbara Hall, the show's creator, deals forthrightly, even didactically, with climate change. Water levels are rising, putting naval bases at risk. Congress denies climate change, despite warnings from the Department of Defense about its effects. Vested interests, including one of the President's donors, are involved in rebuilding the bases in unfriendly countries. He is reluctant to embrace the realities of climate science. But one of the subplots of the show is the President's reelection campaign. Madam Secretary's undaunted desire to "change the world" drives the President to a change of heart. During a debate with his primary opponent, he abruptly announces the reality of climate change and the necessity of taking action. A bold move within the show's narrative; an even bolder one in the narrative of network television, which tends toward middle-of-the-road politics when it deals with politics at all. The President's stand causes him to lose the primary and decide to run as an independent, setting up a continuing plot for the rest of the season.

Where *Veep* presents politics as a profane national travesty and *House of Cards* as the function of a scheming, corrupting intelligence, *Madam Secretary* sees politics as an arena for optimistic action, driven by a strong and undaunted woman. Its premise of quick solutions to intractable political problems is pure fantasy, but a necessary fantasy at the same time. There were, in the recent political world, women Secretaries of State—Madeleine Albright and Hillary Clinton—who had a moral drive and a sense of realpolitik, and *Madam Secretary* is fashioned after them. It gives them and the viewer a gift, that all the problems they couldn't solve could be solved if only in the televisual imagination.

The antidote to fantasy is the daily grind of day-to-day politics—electoral politics, racial politics, gender politics—the spectrum of activity that requires participation, decision making, and a lot of mistakes. Two feature-length HBO films, both directed by Jay Roach, turn politics into semi-fiction—often called "docudramas"—that reimagine signal events in the political universe. One involves the introduction of Sarah Palin into the stew of right-wing politics; the other was the painful birth of the 1965 Civil Rights legislation that gave all African Americans the right to vote—under President Lyndon B. Johnson.

The problem with docudramas involves the limits of imitation and impersonation. How closely to the actual events should the film adhere and how closely to the actual participants should the actors be made up to look? Real-life events, even political ones, are only occasionally dramatic and world-changing. There is much grinding policy work, committee meetings, and conferences; even the rush of political conventions and working on the campaign trail involves a lot of tedium and repetition. A docudrama must spotlight the dramatic moments and make up some to fill the void. Mimicking the looks of the real-life participants is an even trickier proposition. At its best, the mimicking is of mannerisms and speech patterns; at its worst, the actors become waxwork simulations of the people they are playing.

154 Contemporary politics: new channels

Figure 14.3 Morgan Freeman makes a guest appearance with the Secretary of State (Téa Leoni) on *Madam Secretary*.

A fine balance is achieved in *Game Change*, which is based on a political event that was itself highly dramatic and somewhat comic: the selection of Alaska governor Sarah Palin (played with understated mimicry by Julianne Moore) as running mate for the presidential bid of Senator John McCain (Figure 14.4). (The film is based on the book of the same name by political commentators John Heilemann and Mark Halperin.) Palin was a deeply Conservative populist given to odd and fractured statements of her political views. She had a large following of people who thought that bluntness and "straight talking" (often referred to as not being "politically correct") was a refreshing change from the usual and usually evasive political discourse. The problem was that Palin was less than bright and too easy to mock. The fit with the staid and earnest McCain never worked out. The film traces the arc of the campaign, using recreations of events, actual newscasters on cable channels like CNN to report the news of the campaign, and occasionally documentary footage, like a speech delivered by McCain's rival, Barack Obama. In its recreation of the Vice-Presidential debate, the filmmakers intercut actual footage of Joe Biden with Julianne Moore. The result of all this is a remarkably spellbinding film, like watching a trainwreck you know will happen and are helpless to prevent, precisely because it depends on our knowing what will happen.

This is a difficult proposition: if the viewer knows the outcome of an event depicted in a film, it can drain all the expectation and suspense necessary to keep engagement steady. But this is not the case here

Contemporary politics: new channels 155

because Palin was such a polarizing figure of obsessive attention that we want to see *again* how she came into political existence, flaunted her basic ignorance. "Oh my god, what have we done?" cries Steve Schmidt, McCain's campaign advisor played by Woody Harrelson as the team watches the infamous Katie Couric interview in which Palin cannot respond to the question about what newspapers she reads. We know the trainwreck: McCain lost the election. Palin went on to become a figure of admiration on the right and non-stop ridicule from the left. She thrust herself into the political limelight, eclipsed McCain, and became a political joke. She went "rogue," to use the cliché of the moment, and created her own campaign outside of McCain's. The friction provides the film's drama and allowed Roach and his actors to generate a tension of political maneuvering that is irresistible.

Game Change does not make the error of sympathizing with its central characters (though it is definitely on McCain's side), but rather attempts to understand Palin within the context not only of the immediate campaign, but, indirectly, of the political atmosphere of the moment: the collapse of the U.S. economy and the existence of the "Tea Party," the anti-government, anti-spending, populist right for whom Palin became a spokesperson. The filmmakers didn't know it at the time, but Palin was an eerie foreshadowing of Donald J. Trump. As they have McCain say at one point: "There is a dark side to American populism. Some people win elections by tapping into it." McCain refuses to do that and warns Palin not to be coopted by the extremists who would destroy the Republican Party. Palin did not listen and others that followed her did not either. *Game Change* gives an indication

Figure 14.4 John McCain (Ed Harris) introduces his running mate, Sarah Palin (Julianne Moore), in *Game Change*.

of this as the crowd at McCain's concession speech cheers wildly for Palin. She is, indeed, an omen.

All the Way pursues a different path. There is none of the drama of an election and its variety of characters, but rather an attempt to recreate the long process in the struggle for civil rights, focusing on Lyndon Baines Johnson and the passage of the Civil Rights act of 1965. The film has to overcome the immediate burden of impersonation. The characters in *Game Change* suggest, in their appearance, the real-life politicos they represent. Ed Harris, for example, bears a passing resemblance to John McCain. In *All the Way*, Bryan Cranston, fitted out with large prosthetic ears and nose and a receding hairline, looks a bit like a waxwork LBJ (Figure 14.5). One has to get used to this and the other characters impersonating the various historical figures in the drama—Senators Hubert Humphrey and Richard Russell, Martin Luther King—before getting into the rhythm of the film itself, which is more deliberate than *Game Change*. It is the rhythm of hard work in getting a bill passed over overwhelming Southern opposition, focusing on the wheeling and dealing—the difficult, often compromised work of politics. In the course of the film, the work on civil rights legislation is interrupted by the growing crisis in Vietnam, which would ultimately undo Johnson's presidency; the candidacy of a man far to the right, Barry Goldwater; and the despicable head of the FBI, J. Edgar Hoover, who attempts to blackmail Martin Luther King. The film knits these events organically so that they appear as part of the complexity of the political process in which nothing moves smoothly.

Figure 14.5 Lyndon Johnson (Bryan Cranston) confers with Martin Luther King (Anthony Mackie) in *All The Way*.

Johnson is presented as the flawed character he was, someone whose support of African-American rights was compromised by his less than liberal political instincts and fear of losing the South. He is crude and manipulative, by turns bullying and sentimental, committed and disengaged—much like the character portrayed by Robert Caro in his massive, multi-volume biography of Johnson. Johnson prevails, as he did with other important pieces of liberal legislation: the Voting Rights Act of 1965; Medicare and Medicaid; and the food stamp program, among others. *All the Way* becomes a celebration of a brief period in American electoral politics where progressive legislation had a chance of passage. It also darkly predicts the growing strength of Conservatism, which will change the Republican Party and lead to Sarah Palin and Donald J. Trump.

Dramatizing politics is difficult and demanding. Realpolitik, what goes on in the actual world of making deals and laws, can be dramatic and dynamic, even though the political process moves slowly and the political and cultural landscape is strewn with discarded ideas, corrupt individuals, and bad policy. Dramatizing the politics is an act of imaginative elision, concentrating events, refiguring characters, taking the record and turning it into palatable and (perhaps) authentic fiction. The shows and films we have briefly examined try different methods of dramatization, different formal means of addressing political theater.

In the course of our work, we have attempted to look at the spectrum of ways in which the drama of politics is represented in film and television. There are a number of conclusions to be drawn and that should remain with us as we look at the films we discussed and so many others that we haven't. Most important is that "politics" is not an easy concept to define or to represent in film. It stretches from the actions and shenanigans of politicians soliciting our votes and then acting well or badly after they get them. Political movements of the left and right and center are important fodder for political cinema; but whether we consider revolutionary cinema or Hollywood films in which the hero goes against a corrupt corporation or politician, or whether they simply celebrate the family as the safe refuge in a chaotic world, we need to pay attention to the ways in which the films are telling their story and what they expect of us, their audience. We have discussed the politics of form and content, but we also need to consider the politics of *reception*. How do we respond to political films? For example, is your mind changed about the Cuban Revolution after watching *Lucía*? What is your opinion about Fascism, having discussed *Triumph of the Will* and *The Conformist*? How do you compare the arguments about race in such different works as Griffith's *The Birth of a Nation* and Edelman's *O. J.: Made in America*?

Perhaps seeing the films discussed in this book has made you want to see more and think differently about the films or television you see. If so, it would be useful to think about what you mean by entertainment or, even more precisely, how you respond to unusual formal and thematic elements in film and television. We've talked about the idea of making films politically, and it might be important, as we conclude, to think about *viewing* films politically. Perhaps the ultimate goal of this book and the films we've examined is to end the innocence of film or television viewing, to understand that whatever a work of simple entertainment or outright propaganda has to say, you need to interpret both what it is saying and how it is saying it. Like it or not, we are all political animals; we are subject to politics and, even on the micro level, we practice politics in our daily lives.

Notes

1 https://en.wikiquote.org/wiki/House_of_Cards_(U.S._TV_series)#Chapter_44_.5B4.05.5D.
2 Shortly after this was written, actor Kevin Spacey faced allegations of sexual misconduct. He was fired from the show and future seasons of *House of Cards* are uncertain.

Further reading

Fredric Jameson, *The Political Unconscious: Narrative as a Socially Symbolic Act* (Ithaca, NY: Cornell University Press, 1981).

Jeffery P. Jones, *Entertaining Politics: New Political Television and Civic Culture* (Lanham, MD: Rowman & Littlefield Publishers, 2004).

Chuck Tryon, *Political TV* (New York and London: Routledge, 2016).

Bibliography

Jonathan Auerbach, "Looking in: McKinley at Home," *Body Shots: Early Cinema's Incarnations* (Berkeley, CA: University of California Press, 2007).
Steven Bach, *Leni: The Life and Work of Leni Riefenstahl* (New York: Alfred A. Knopf, 2007).
Donald Bogle, *Toms, Coons, Mulattoes, Mammies, and Bucks: An Interpretive History of Blacks in American Films* (London, New Delhi, New York, and Sydney: Bloomsbury Academic, 2015).
David Bordwell, Janet Staiger, Kristin Thompson, *The Classical Hollywood Cinema* (New York: Columbia University Press, 1987).
Pearl Bowser, Jane Gaines, Charles Musser, eds., *Oscar Micheaux and His Circle: African-American Filmmaking and Race Cinema of the Silent Era* (Bloomington and Indianapolis, IN: Indiana University Press, 2001).
Michael Broderick, *Reconstructing Strangelove: Inside Stanley Kubrick's 'Nightmare Comedy'* (New York: Columbia University Press, 2017).
Richard Brody, *Everything is Cinema: The Working Life of Jean-Luc Godard* (New York: Metropolitan Books, 2008).
Robert Burgoyne, *Film Nation: Hollywood Looks at U.S. History* (Minneapolis, MN and London: University of Minneapolis Press, 1997).
Julianne Burton, ed., *Cinema and Social Change in Latin America: Conversations with Filmmakers* (Austin, TX: University of Texas Press, 1986).
Frank Capra, *The Name Above the Title: An Autobiography* (New York: Da Capo Press, 1997).
Larry Ceplair and Steven Englund, *The Inquisition in Hollywood: Politics in the Film Community, 1930–1960* (Berkeley and Los Angeles, CA and London: University of California Press, 1983).
Michael Chanon, *The Cuban Image* (London and Bloomington, IN: BFI Publishing and University of Indiana Press, 1985).
—— *Cultural Studies of the Americas: Cuban Cinema* (Minneapolis, MN: University of Minnesota Press, 2004).
James Combs, *Movies and Politics: The Dynamic Relationship* (New York and London: Garland Publishing, 1993).

Thomas Cripps, *Slow Fade to Black: The Negro in American Film, 1900–1942* (New York: Oxford University Press, 1977).
Gary Crowdus, "Terrorism and Torture in *The Battle of Algiers*: An Interview with Saadi Yacef," *Cinéaste*, Vol. 29, No. 3 (Summer 2004), 30–37.
Terry Eagleton, *Ideology* (London and New York: Verso, 1991).
Sergei Eisenstein, *The Film Sense*, ed. and trans. Jay Leyda (New York: Harcourt Brace Jovanovich, 1975).
——— *The Film Form: Essays in Film Theory*, ed. and trans. Jay Leyda (San Diego, CA: Harcourt Brace Jovanovich, 1977).
Frantz Fanon, *The Wretched of the Earth*, trans. Constance Farrington (New York: Grove Press, 1963), 35.
——— *A Dying Colonialism*, trans. Haakon Chevalier (New York: Grove Press, 1965), 44, 48.
Fabian Gerard, T. Jefferson Kline, Bruce Sklarew, eds., *Berolucci: Interviews* (Oxford, MS: University of Mississippi Press, 2000).
Richard Giglio, *Here's Looking at You: Hollywood, Film and Politics*, 4th ed. (New York: Peter Lang Publishing, 2014).
Barry Keith Grant, *Invasion of the Body Snatchers* (London: BFI and Palgrave Macmillan, 2010).
J. Ronald Green, *Straight Lick: The Cinema of Oscar Micheaux* (Bloomington, IN: University of Indiana Press, 2000).
Ed Guerrero, *Framing Blackness* (Philadelphia, PA: Temple University Press, 1993).
Tom Gunning, *D. W. Griffith and the Origins of American Narrative Film: The Early Years at Biograph* (Urbana and Chicago, IL: University of Illinois Press, 1991).
Mark Harris, *Five Came Back: A Story of Hollywood and the Second World War* (New York: Penguin Random House, 2015).
Sylvia Harvey, *May '68 and Film Culture* (London: BFI Publishing, 1980).
Margot Henriksen, *Dr. Strangelove's America: Society and Culture in the Atomic Age* (Berkeley and Los Angeles, CA and London: University of California Press, 1997).
J. Hoberman, *An Army of Phantoms: American Movies and the Making of the Cold War* (New York: New Press, 2011).
Richard Hofstadter, *The Paranoid Style in American Politics, and Other Essays* (New York: Vintage Books, 2008), 23–24.
Fredric Jameson, *The Political Unconscious: Narrative as a Socially Symbolic Act* (Ithaca, NY: Cornell University Press, 1981).
Jeffery P. Jones, *Entertaining Politics: New Political Television and Civic Culture* (Lanham, MD: Rowman & Littlefield Publishers, 2004).
Robert P. Kolker, *Bertolucci* (London: The British Film Institute, 1985).
——— *The Altering Eye: Contemporary International Cinema* (Cambridge, UK: Open Book Publishers, 2009), https://doi.org/10.11647/OBP.0002.
——— *A Cinema of Loneliness*, 4th ed. (New York: Oxford University Press, 2011).

Peter Krämer, *Dr. Strangelove or: How I Learned to Stop Worrying and Love the Bomb* (London: BFI and Palgrave Macmillan, 2014).

Frank Krutnik, Steve Neale, Brian Neve, Peter Stanfield, eds., *'Un-American' Hollywood: Politics and Film in the Blacklist Era* (New Brunswick, NJ: Rutgers University Press, 2007).

Marcia Landy, ed., *Imitations of Life: A Reader on Film and Television Melodrama*, ed. Marcia Landy (Detroit, MI: Wayne State University Press, 1991).

Jackson Lears, *Rebirth of a Nation: The Making of Modern America, 1877–1920* (New York: Harper Collins, 2009).

Primo Levi, *Survival in Auschwitz: The Nazi Assault on Humanity*, trans. Stuart Woolf (New York: Touchstone, 1996).

Jon Lewis, "'We Do Not Ask You to Condone This': How the Blacklist Saved Hollywood," *Cinema Journal*, Vol. 39 (2000), 3–30.

Katrina Mann, "'You're Next!': Postwar Hegemony Besieged in *Invasion of the Body Snatchers*," *Cinema Journal*, Vol. 44, No. 1 (2004), 49–68.

Davin Mayer, *Sergei M. Eisenstein's Potemkin: A Shot-by-Shot Presentation* (New York: Grossman, 1972).

Ewa Mazierska, *European Cinema and Intertextuality: History, Memory and Politics* (London: Palgrave Macmillan, 2011).

Joseph McBride, *Frank Capra: The Catastrophe of Success* (New York: Simon and Schuster, 1992).

Joan Mellon, *Filmguide to The Battle of Algiers* (Bloomington, IN: Indiana University Press, 1973).

Tom Milne, ed. and trans., *Godard on Godard* (New York: Da Capo Press, 1986).

James Monaco, *The New Wave: Truffaut, Godard, Chabrol, Rohmer, Rivette* (Sag Harbor, NY: Harbor Electronic Publishing, 2004).

John Mraz, "*Lucia*: Visual Style and Historical Portrayal," *Jump Cut*, 19 (December 1978), www.ejumpcut.org/archive/jc50.2008/Lucia.

Victor S. Navasky, *Naming Names*, 3rd ed. (New York: Hill and Wang, 2003).

Monica White Ndounou, *Shaping the Future of African American Film: Color-Coded Economics and the Story Behind the Numbers* (New Brunswick, NJ: Rutgers University Press, 2014).

Richard Neupert, *A History of the French New Wave Cinema* (Madison, WI: University of Wisconsin Press, 2002).

Bill Nichols, *Representing Reality: Issues and Concepts in Documentary* (Bloomington, IN: Indiana University Press, 1991).

——— *Introduction to Documentary* (Bloomington, IN: Indiana University Press, 2001).

David Overby, trans. and ed., *Springtime in Italy: A Reader on Neo-Realism* (Hamden, CT: Archon Books, 1979).

Constance Penley, ed., *Close Encounters: Film, Feminism, and Science Fiction Film* (Minneapolis, MN: University of Minnesota Press, 1991).

Dušan Radunović, "The Shifting Protocols of the Visible: The Becoming of Sergei Eisenstein's *The Battleship Potemkin*," *Film History: An International Journal*, Vol. 29, No. 2 (2017), 66–90.

Jeffery Richards, "Frank Capra and the Cinema of Populism," in Bill Nichols, ed., *Movies and Methods*, Vol. 1 (Berkeley and Los Angeles, CA: University of California Press, 1976), 65–77.

Richard Rushton, *The Politics of Hollywood Cinema: Popular Film and Contemporary Political Theory* (London: Palgrave Macmillan, 2013).

David Seed, *American Science Fiction and the Cold War: Literature and Film* (Chicago, IL: Fitzroy Dearborn, 1999).

Tony Shaw, *Cinematic Terror: A Global History of Terrorism on Film* (New York: Bloomsbury, 2014).

William Shirer, *The Rise and Fall of the Third Reich: A History of Nazi Germany* (New York: Simon & Schuster, 1959, 2011).

Robert Sklar and Vito Zagarrio, eds., *Frank Capra: Authorship and the Studio System* (Philadelphia, PA: Temple University Press, 1998).

Vivian Sobchack, *Screening Space: The American Science Fiction Film*, 2nd ed. (New York: Ungar, 1987).

Melvyn Stokes, *D. W. Griffith's* The Birth of a Nation: *A History of 'The Most Controversial Motion Picture of All Time'* (New York: Oxford University Press, 2007).

Frances Stonor-Saunders, *The Cultural Cold War: The CIA and the World of Arts and Letters* (New York and London: The New Press, 2015).

J. P. Telotte, *Science Fiction Film* (New York: Cambridge University Press, 2001).

Claretta Tonetti, *Bernardo Bertolucci: The Cinema of Ambiguity* (Woodbridge, CT: Twayne Publisher, 2005).

Robert Brent Toplin, *Oliver Stone's USA: Film, History, and Controversy* (Lawrence, KS: University of Kansas Press, 2000).

Jürgen Trimborn, *Leni Riefenstahl: A Life* (Faber & Faber, Inc., 2002, translated by Edna McCown in 2007).

Chuck Tryon, *Political TV* (New York and London: Routledge, 2016).

Karen Wieland, *Dietrich and Riefenstahl: Hollywood, Berlin, and a Century of Two Lives*, trans. Shelley Frisch (New York: Liverwight, 2011).

John Willett, ed. and trans., *Brecht on Theatre: The Development of an Aesthetic* (New York: Hill and Wand, 1992).

Woodrow Wilson, *A History of the American People*, Vol. LX (New York: Harper & Brothers, 1918 [originally published 1901]).

Index

12 Years a Slave 144
13th 144
2001: A Space Odyssey 106

agitprop 25, 84, 91
Albright, Madeleine 153
Alea, Tomás Gutiérrez 80
Alexander Nevsky 36
Algerian Revolution 59–69
All the President's Men 132
All the Way 149, 156–7
Allen, Woody 36
Althusser, Louis 2
American Madness 49
American Mutoscope and Biograph Company *see* Biograph company
An American Tragedy 36
The Americans 149
António das Mortes 70
Antonioni, Michelangelo 94, 136–7
Apartheid 60
apocalyptic films 81–92
artificiality 73, 84
assassination, *JFK* 131–8
Association of Motion Picture Producers 123
Auden, W. H. 105
auteur theory 81–2
avant-garde cinema 25, 35, 93, 134
L'avventura 94

Bacon, Francis 33
Balsamo, Joseph 88
Bananas 36
Barbershop series 144–5
Batista, Fulgencio 72, 76

The Battle of Algiers 59–69, 70, 125
Battleship Potemkin 24–37, 79, 83, 125
Bazin, André 82
Berlin Olympics 45
Bertolucci, Bernardo 94–101
Bessie, Alvah 123
Biberman, Herbert J. 123, 124, 126
Bicycle Thieves 61–2
Big Jim McLain 105
Bigelow, Kathryn 143
bildungsroman 86
Biograph company 11, 13
The Birth of a Nation 7, 9–23, 25, 26–7, 46, 79, 143, 144, 148; Parker's version 21–2
Bitzer, Billy 11
Blake, William 86
Blaxploitation 144
Blow-Up 94, 136–7
The Blue Light 40
Body Snatchers 109
Bonnie and Clyde 86
Brando, Marlon 101
The Brave One 124
Brazil 70
Breathless 84
Brecht, Bertolt 36, 71, 82, 84, 89–90, 124
The Bridge on the River Kwai 124
Bridge of Spies 5
Buñuel, Luis 88
Bush, George W. 140–1, 143

Caché (Hidden) 61
Cantata de Chile 80

Index

capitalism 3, 11, 24, 26, 38, 48, 130
Capra, Frank 46, 48–58, 86, 150
"Capracorn" 52, 57
Carmichael, Stokely 90
Castro, Fidel 72, 78
CBS 149
Ceplair, Larry 122
Chabrol, Claude 82
Chambers, Whittaker 104, 121
Chaplin, Charlie 36
Chile 70, 80
Cinema Novo 70
cinéma vérité 139
Citizen Kane 83
Civil Rights Act 149, 153, 156–7
Civil Rights movement 103, 144, 145
Civil War 13–15, 19, 20
The Clansman 13
Classical Hollywood Style 6, 26–7, 29, 50, 79, 134
Clinton, Hillary 153
Cohn, Roy 111, 112–13
Cold War 5; *The Americans* 149; *Dr. Strangelove* 111–19; *Invasion of the Body Snatchers* 102–10; paranoia 130, 131; *Point of Order* 111–19
Cole, Lester 123
colonialism 59–68
Communism 2, 24, 38–40, 87; Cuba 71; U.S. anti-Communism 5, 71, 102–9, 111–19, 120–5, 128–9, 130, 131
computer-generated imagery (CGI) 26
The Conformist 93–101
conspiracy theories 130–1
Contempt 84
Cooper, Gary 121
Corner in Wheat 11–12, 13, 25, 26, 49
Couric, Katie 155
Cuba 71–80; missile crisis 114
Cukor, George 19
Curtiz, Michael 122

Da Sweet Blood of Jesus 144
Dadaism 93
Dassin, Jules 124

The Day the Earth Stood Still 106
de Antonio, Emile 111–13, 139, 140
De Palma, Brian 36
De Sica, Vittorio 61
Delerue, Georges 95
democracy 68, 70, 93; liberal 2, 3; U.S. 48–58, 59, 151
Depression 48–9, 56
dialectics 24
"Dickens, Griffith, and the Film Today" 25–6
Dickson, W. K. L. 9, 11
Dies, Martin 120
Disney Studios 56, 121, 145
Disney, Walt 36, 121
Dixon, Thomas 13
Dmytryk, Edward 123
Do the Right Thing 144
docudramas 153–7
documentaries 139–48, see also *Triumph of the Will*
domino theory 142
Douglas, Kirk 124
Dr. Strangelove or: How I Learned to Stop Worrying and Love the Bomb 92, 111–19
Dreiser, Theodore 36
Drew, Robert 139
Dumas, Alexandre 88
DuVernay, Ava 144

Eagleton, Terry 2
Edelman, Ezra 7, 145–8
Edison, Thomas 9
Eisenhower, Dwight David 133
Eisenstein, Sergei 25–6, 27–36, 83, 133
Eliot, T. S. 83–4
Engels, 90
Englund, Steven 122
Exodus 124
The Exterminating Angel 88

Fahrenheit 9/11 140–1
Fanon, Frantz 60, 63–4, 90
Fascism 2, 24, 38–47, 48, 49, 89, 118–19, 148; *The Conformist* 93–101; Italy 39, 61, 93, 99, see also Nazism
Fellini, Federico 94

Ferdinand, Archduke 131, 132
Ferrara, Abel 109
Fetchit, Stepin 19, 143
film noir 57, 83
Fisher, Frederick 112–13
Fleming, Victor 19
The Fog of War: Eleven Lessons from the Life of Robert S. McNamara 142–3
For Whom the Bell Tolls 39
Forbidden Planet 106
France 9–10, 95; Algerian Revolution 60–1, 63–5, 67–8; French Revolution 88, 89; *Last Tango in Paris* 95, 101; Tradition of Quality 81, 82; *Weekend* 81–92
Franco, General Francisco 39
Frankenheimer, John 131
futurism 93–4, 105–6

Game Change 149, 154–6
gangster films 5, 82, 84
Garrison, Jim 134–6, 137
Geer, Will 125
gender 84; Algerian Revolution 63–4, 65; Cuba 72–3, 78–9; Nazism 42–3; *Salt of the Earth* 125–8
George, Peter 114
Gibney, Alex 141
Giral, Sergio 71–2
Godard, Jean-Luc 68, 82, 83–92, 95
Goebbels, Joseph 40
Gold Diggers 49
Goldwater, Barry 156
Goldwyn, Samuel 122
Gone with the Wind 19–21
Gore, Al 140
Griffith, D. W. 10–12, 13–21, 22, 25–6, 46, 49, 143
Guernica 39
Guevara, Alfredo 71
Gypsy concentration camps 45

Halperin, Mark 154
Haneke, Michael 61
Haskin, Byron 106
Hawks, Howard 106
HBO 145, 149, 153
Hegel, 24

Heilemann, John 154
Hellman, Lillian 104
Hemingway, Ernest 39
Hess, Rudolf 43
Hetherington, Tim 141
Himmler, Heinrich 43
Hirschbiegel, Oliver 109
Hiss, Alger 104, 121
Hitchcock, Alfred 82, 105
Hitler, Adolf 24, 39–45, 48, 93, 103
Hitler Youth 42
Hofstadter, Richard 130
Hoover, J. Edgar 156
House of Cards 149, 150–1, 153, 158n1–2
House Committee on Un-American Activities (HUAC) 104, 105, 120–5, 128–9
Hughes, Howard 124
Humphrey, Hubert 139, 156
The Hunger Games 6
Hunter, Ian McLellan 124
The Hurt Locker 143

I Am a Fugitive from a Chain Gang 48–9
I Married a Communist 124
illusion-making 27
India, colonialism 60
Instituto Cubano de Arte e Industria Cinematográficos (ICAIC) 71, 72, 80
intellectual montage 28
International Alliance of Theatrical Stage Employees 125
International Union of Mine, Mill and Smelter Workers 125
Intolerance 19
The Invasion 109
Invasion of the Body Snatchers 102–10
Iraq War 140–1, 143
It Happened One Night 49, 86
Italy 93–101; Fascism 39, 61, 93, 99; neorealism 61–2, 66, 70, 71, 81, 94, 99, 124, 125, 136
It's a Wonderful Life 49–50, 57
Ivan the Terrible 36

Jarrico, Paul 124–5
Jews 31, 40, 44, 93, 102, 120

JFK 130–8
Johnson, Lyndon 142, 149, 153, 156–7
Joyce, James 83
Junger, Sebastian 141

Kahn, Herman 114
Kaufman, Denis *see* Vertov, Dziga
Kaufman, Philip 109
Kazan, Elia 123, 129
Kennan, George 103
Kennedy, John F. 114; *JFK* 130–8; *Primary* 139
The Killing 5
King, Martin Luther 146, 156
King, Rodney 146
kino eye 25, 28, 139
Kino Pravda 25
Kissinger, Henry 117
Korean War 103, 131
Ku Klux Klan 13, 17–18, 120
Kubrick, Stanley 5, 92, 106, 114–16, 118–19, 124
"Kuleshov effect" 27
Kuleshov, Lev 25, 27

Lang, Fritz 105–6
Langlois, Henri 82
Lardner, Ring Jr 123
The Last Emperor 101
Last Tango in Paris 95, 101
Lawrence of Arabia 124
Lawrence, Francis 6
Lawrence, Jennifer 6
Lawson, John Howard 123
Léaud, Jean-Pierre 89
Lee, Malcolm D. 145
Lee, Spike 144
LeMay, Curtis 116
Lenin, Vladimir 24
LeRoy, Mervyn 48–9
Levi, Primo 40
liberal democracy 2, 3
Lincoln, Abraham 14, 39
Lincoln Motion Picture Company 19
Losey, Joseph 124
Lowlands 45
Lucas, George 46, 106
Lucía 70–80, 125
Lumière Brothers 10

McCain, John 149, 154–6
McCarey, Leo 105
McCarthy, Joseph 104, 111–13, 118, 121, 131
McDaniel, Hattie 20, 143
Machado, Gerardo 72, 76
McKinley, William 10, 11, 139
McNamara, Robert S. 142–3
McQueen, Butterfly 20
McQueen, Steve 144
Madam Secretary 149, 151–4
Madden, John 57
Malcom X 144
Maltz, Albert 123
Man with a Movie Camera 25, 139
The Manchurian Candidate 131
Marinetti, Filippo 94
Marshall Plan 103
Marx, Karl 24, 36, 38, 89
Marxism 2, 24, 26, 28, 36, 38, 84, 86, 87, 89
Mean Streets 5
Meet John Doe 49
Mein Kampf 39
Metropolis 105–6
MGM 106, 122
Micheaux, Oscar 19
Milestone, Lewis 122
mise-en-scène 73, 106
Miss Sloane 57
Mission to Moscow 122
modernism 83, 93–4
modernity 9, 82–3
montage 25–32, 35–6, 126, 132; Capra films 51–2, 56; intellectual 28; parallel editing 11, 18, 25–6; Stone films 133–4
Moore, Michael 139–41
Morris, Errol 141–3
Motion Picture Alliance for the Preservation of American Ideals 121–2
Mr. Smith Goes to Washington 48–58, 59, 79, 135, 150
Murrow, Edward R. 112
Mussolini, Benito 39, 61, 93, 99
Mutually Assured Destruction (MAD) 114, 115
My Life to Live 84
My Son John 105

Naked City 124
National Association for the Advancement of Colored People (NAACP) 18
Nazis/Nazism 18, 38, 39–48, 56, 81, 102–3, 111, 148; *Dr. Strangelove* 117–18; HUAC 120, 122; *Rome, Open City* 66; *Triumph of the Will* 7, 38–47, 79, 94, 139
neorealism 61–2, 66, 70, 71, 81, 94, 99, 124, 125, 136
Netflix 144, 149, 152
New Wave 82, 83, 89, 92
Nixon 137
Nixon, Richard 104, 121, 131–2, 137
North Star 122
nuclear weapons 103, 104, 105, 114–18, 130
Nuremburg rally 41–4
Nyby, Christian 106

O. J.: Made in America 7, 145–8, 149
Obama, Barack 154
October: Ten Days That Shook the World 28, 35
Old and New 28
Olympia 45
On Thermonuclear War 114
On the Waterfront 123
Operation Abolition 128–9
Ornitz, Samuel 123
Oswald, Lee Harvey 132, 134, 136
The Other Francisco 71–2
Out 1 82

Pakula, Alan J. 132
Palin, Sarah 153–6, 157
The Parallax View 132
parallel editing 11, 18, 25–6
Paramount 36, 121
The Paranoid Style in American Politics 130
Paris Cinématèque 82
Parker, Nate 21–2
Parks, Gordon 144
Parnell Thomas, J. 123
Pasolini, Pier Paolo 94
Pearl Harbor 56–7
Penn, Arthur 86

Perry, Tyler 144
Picasso, Pablo 39
Pinochet, Augusto 70
Planet of the Apes 124
Plato 95, 96, 100
Point of Order 111–19, 139, 140
Pontecorvo, Gillo 61, 65–8
populism 24, 26, 38–9, 46, 79, 113; *The Birth of a Nation* 9–23; Capra 49–50, 51, 57; U.S. 122, 131, 154–5
Prelude to War 56–7
Preminger, Otto 124
Primary 139
Production Code 121
Progressive Era 13
Pudovkin, Vsevolod 25
Pulp Fiction 4–6

¡*Qué viva México!* 35–6

race/racism 7, 9, 13–14, 16–22, 27, 31, 143–8, see also *The Birth of a Nation*; Nazism
Rankin, John 120
Rapper, Irving 124
Ratoff, Gregory 122
realpolitik 38, 153, 157
Rear Window 105
Reconstruction 13, 16, 20
Red Alert 114
Red Desert 94
Restrepo 141
Revueltas, Rosaura 125
Riefenstahl, Leni 38–47, 94, 139
Rivette, Jacques 82
RKO 124
Roach, Jay 153, 155
road movies 86, 97
Rocha, Glauber 70
Röhm, Ernst 41
Rohmer, Eric 82
Roman Holiday 124
Rome, Open City 61–2, 66
Roosevelt, Franklin Delano 48, 56, 102, 103
Rosenberg, Ethel and Julius 102, 104, 112
Rossellini, Roberto 61–2, 66
Russell, Richard 156

Index

Salt of the Earth 120–9
Sanders, Bernie 2
satire 86, 111, 114–15, 117
Schine, G. David 111
Schmidt, Steve 155
Schulberg, Budd 123
science fiction 102–10
Scorsese, Martin 5
Scott, Adrian 123
The Searchers 105
Sellers, Peter 115, 116, 117, 118
Selma 144
Selznick, David O. 21
September 11th terrorist attacks 140–1
Shaft 144
Shaw, Clay 134, 136
Siegel, Don 106, 108
Simpson, O. J. 7, 145
slavery 13–14, 19–22, 56, 59, 60, 71–2, 148; *12 Years a Slave* 144; *Slaves* 124
Slaves 124
Snowden, Edward 120
Socialist Realism 35, 93
Solás, Humberto 72–80
Song of Russia 122, 124
Sontag, Susan 44–5
South Africa, colonialism 60
Southern, Terry 114–15
Soviet Union 102–5, 139; Cuban missile crisis 114; *Dr. Strangelove* 92, 111–19; Hollywood films 122; *Man with a Movie Camera* 25, 139; Russian Revolution 24–37; Socialist Realism 35, 93, *see also* Cold War
Spacey, Kevin 151, 152, 158n2
Spartacus 124
The Spider's Stratagem 95, 101
Spielberg, Steven 5
Stalin, Josef 24, 35–6, 38, 102–3, 122
Standard Operating Procedure 142
Star Wars 46, 106
Stevens, Thaddeus 14
Stevenson, Adlai 116
Stevenson, Robert 124
Stone, Oliver 133–7
Storaro, Vittorio 95

Story, Tim 145
Strawberry and Chocolate 80
Strike 28
Sturmabteilung 41
Sullivan, Kevin Rodney 145
Surrealism 88, 93
Sweet Sweetback's Baadasssss Song 144

Tabío, Juan Carlos 80
Tarantino, Quentin 5–6
Taxi to the Dark Side 141
television films and series 7–8, 145–8, 149–58
The Thing from Another World 106
Tisse, Eduard 28
torture 66
totalitarianism 24, 36, 38, 108
Tradition of Quality 81, 82
treason 120
Trintignant, Jean-Louis 95, 96, 98
Triumph of the Will 7, 38–47, 79, 94, 139
Truffaut, François 82
Truman Doctrine 103
Truman, Harry 103
Trumbo, Dalton 123, 124
Trump, Donald J. 2, 3, 112, 155, 157
Turner, Nat 22

United States: anti-Communism 5, 71, 102–9, 111–19, 120–5, 128–9, 130, 131; Blaxploitation 144; Cuban missile crisis 114; documentaries 139–48; *Dr. Strangelove* 92, 111–19; *Fahrenheit 9/11* 140–1; *The Fog of War* 142–3; Hollywood Blacklist 120–9; Iraq War 140–1, 143; *JFK* 130–8; *O. J.: Made in America* 7, 145–8, 149; *Point of Order* 111–19, 139, 140; *Primary* 139, *see also The Birth of a Nation*; Cold War
The Untouchables 36

Van Peebles, Melvin 144
Veep 149–50, 151–2, 153

vertical integration 121
Vertov, Dziga 25, 27–8, 139
Victory of Faith 41
Vietnam War 61, 65, 70, 82, 84, 112, 116, 133, 135–6, 156; *The Fog of War* 142–3; *JFK* 133
Visconti, Luchino 94
von Braun, Werner 117
Vorkapich, Slavko 51

War of the Worlds 106
Warhol, Andy 83
Warner Bros. 48–9, 121, 122
Warner, Jack 121
Warren Commission 132
Wayne, John 105, 121
Weekend 81–92
Welles, Orson 36, 83

Wellman, William A. 48
Welsh, Joseph 112–13
Westerns 105
white supremacists 26, 120, *see also* Ku Klux Klan
Why We Fight 56
Wilcox, Fred 106
Wild Boys of the Road 48
Wilson, Michael 124
Wilson, Woodrow 18
Within Our Gates 19
The Woman on Pier 13 124
World War II: aftermath 102–3; Hollywood 121
Wyler, William 124

Zapruder, Abraham 134, 136
Zombie movies 4, 91, 109

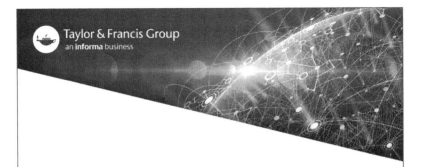